Schüler-Lernkrimi Englisch

Ultimatum by SMS

John William Holway

Compact Verlag

Bisher sind in dieser Reihe erschienen:
- Englisch, Französisch, Spanisch, Latein, Deutsch, Mathematik, Physik, Chemie

In der Reihe Compact Lernkrimi sind erschienen:
- Englisch, Französisch, Italienisch, Spanisch: B1, B2
- Englisch GB/US, Business English: B1, B2
- Deutsch: B1
- Sammelband Lernkrimi Englisch: B1/B2

In der Reihe Compact Lernkrimi Kurzkrimis sind erschienen:
- Englisch, Französisch, Italienisch, Spanisch, Deutsch: A2

In der Reihe Compact Lernkrimi History sind erschienen:
- Englisch: B1, B2, Italienisch: B1

In der Reihe Compact Lernthriller sind erschienen:
- Englisch: B1, B2, Spanisch: B1

In der Reihe Compact Lernstory Mystery sind erschienen:
- Englisch: B1, B2

In der Reihe Compact Lernkrimi Hörbuch sind erschienen:
- Englisch: B1, B2, Business English: B2
- Französisch, Italienisch, Spanisch: B1

In der Reihe Compact Lernkrimi Audio-Learning sind erschienen:
- Englisch: A2, B1

Lernziele:
- Grundwortschatz, Grammatik (A2, B1)
- Aufbauwortschatz, Konversation (B2)

Weitere Titel sind in Vorbereitung.

Chefredaktion: Dr. Angela Sendlinger
Redaktion: Patrizia Ginocchio
Fachredaktion: Fiona Cain
Produktion: Wolfram Friedrich
Illustrationen: Doris Oppenauer
Titelillustration: Karl Knospe
Typographischer Entwurf: Maria Seidel
Umschlaggestaltung: Inga Koch

ISBN 978-3-8174-7823-1
7278231

Besuchen Sie uns im Internet: www.compactverlag.de, www.lernkrimi.de

Vorwort

Mit dem neuen, spannenden Compact Schüler-Lernkrimi könnt ihr eure Englischkenntnisse auf schnelle und einfache Weise vertiefen, auffrischen und überprüfen.

Die Freunde Susan, Heather, Tracey, George und Arthur erleichtern das Sprachtraining mit Action und Humor. Die fünf und ihre spannenden Erlebnisse rund um das verschwundene Medaillon stehen im Mittelpunkt einer geheimnisvollen Story.

Der Krimi wird auf jeder Seite durch abwechslungsreiche und kurzweilige Übungen ergänzt, die das Lernen unterhaltsam und spannend machen.

Prüfe dein Englisch in Lückentexten, Zuordnungsaufgaben, in Wahr-oder-Falsch-Übungen und Buchstabenspielen!

Dieses Sprachtraining im handlichen Format bietet mit 60 Übungen die ideale Trainingsmöglichkeit für zwischendurch. Schreibe die Lösungen einfach ins Buch!

Die richtigen Antworten sind in einem eigenen Lösungsteil zusammengefasst. Im Anhang steht außerdem ein Glossar, in dem die schwierigsten Wörter übersetzt sind. Diese sind im Text kursiv markiert.

Und nun kann die Spannung beginnen ...

Viel Spaß und Erfolg!

Inhalt

Story

Nach einem Hockeyspiel in der Schule ist plötzlich Susans Medaillon aus der Umkleidekabine verschwunden. Susan ist außer sich, denn das Medaillon ist ein Erbstück ihrer Großmutter, das ihr sehr viel bedeutet. Kurz darauf bekommt sie eine mysteriöse SMS mit der Forderung, bis Ende der Woche £200 zu zahlen und niemandem davon zu erzählen. Falls sie sich nicht an die Abmachung halten sollte, würde sie ihr Medaillon nie wieder sehen.
Wer steckt hinter dem Diebstahl? Und aus welchem Grund? Susan hat eine Vermutung. Gemeinsam mit ihren Freunden Tracey, Heather, George und Arthur versucht sie den Dieb zu fassen – eine mehr als abenteuerliche Aufgabe.
Wird es ihnen gelingen den wahren Dieb zu stellen?

Chapter 1: The Winning Shot

Holding her stick firmly in both hands, Susan raced down the side of the hockey field. She was determined to reach the goal *at all costs*. Faster and faster she ran and her heart beat wildly. It was a glorious day at St. Mary's and the sun shone brightly from a cloudless sky. Her friends *cheered* from the sidelines "Susan, Susan" and she felt *pride rise up* in her *chest*. Although she was only 15, Susan was the captain of the senior hockey team at St. Mary's High School and hockey was her greatest love. Today was the final match of the season against their local rivals Merrywood School and there was still no score.

There were only five minutes left to play and Susan felt that she just had to make it all the way to the goal. Her parents had also come to watch today and she knew they simply had to win. She felt that everything depended on her. All eyes were now on her as she quickly *steered* the hockey ball down the side of the hockey field towards the goal. Over her shoulder one of the Merrywood *defenders* raced to try to catch Susan, but Susan was much faster.

Then suddenly in front of her came the final Merrywood *defender*, a big blonde girl built like an *ox*. The girl was *convinced* she would block Susan, but Susan had other ideas. Quickly she moved to the right, then back to the left and in an instant she was past the *defender* with only the *goalkeeper* to beat.

With a *keen* eye she focused on the goal, then she swung back her stick and with a *whack* sound the stick crashed against the leather of the ball. The ball *sailed* high and into the top right-hand corner of the net. Cheers went up from around the ground:

"Goal, goal, goal! Hooray, hooray, hooray," but Susan let out a scream of pain and fell to the grass.

"Agh, my leg, my leg," she cried.

ÜBUNG 1 !

Übung 1: Unterstreiche die sechs Wörter, die falsch geschrieben sind, und verbessere sie!

In her efforts to *score* the gole she had stretched aut her leg too far and *torn* a *muscle* in her rite leg. A fire burnt in the *calf* of her leg and she rolled in paine on the ground. Susan was a brave fighter, but she fellt the emotions *well up* inside of her and teers of pain rolled down her cheeks.

1. ______________ 4. ______________

2. ______________ 5. ______________

3. ______________ 6. ______________

Quickly she tried to *fight off* the tears and *wiped* her streaming eyes with her *muddy* hands.
The team coach Mrs Hiller made her way through the crowd that was now *gathering* around Susan.
"Let me through, out of the way," she cried as she pushed the players to the side and *knelt* down beside Susan.
"Where does it hurt? Are you alright, Susan?" she asked in a *compassionate* voice.
In Susan's mind there was only one question:
"Did I *score*? Did I get the goal?"
"Yes, yes," replied Mrs Hiller. "Super goal, well done, my dear, you won the match. Now about your leg, where does it hurt?"
In her moment of triumph Susan had completely forgotten about the pain: she had won the match! Her shot had *scored* a goal and St. Mary's had won! As she looked up she saw a sea of faces around her. Her own *team mates* and even some of the Merrywood girls were *gazing* down at her.

"Give the girl some *space*!" shouted Mrs Hiller. "She needs to breathe and get some fresh air."

Übung 2: Lies weiter und ordne die Buchstaben zu einem sinnvollen Wort!

ÜBUNG 2 !

By now (1. eth) ____________ *referee* and several parents had arrived to push back the *onlookers* and to (2. kame) ____________ *space* for Susan to be treated.

"It's my right leg," said Susan. "I think I (3. veha) ____________ *torn* the *calf muscle*."

"Let me see," said Mrs Hiller as she gently (4. tlef) ____________ the muscles in Susan's right (5. gel) ____________.

"Ooh, ahh," cried Susan as she felt the (6. aipn) ____________ shoot through her leg.

"Give me the *sponge*," said Mrs Hiller and *squeezed* cold (7. awter) ____________ over the back of Susan's leg.

Immediately Susan felt *relief* as the cold water *eased the pain*. Again Mrs Hiller gently pressed on the *calf* muscle before announcing:
"Yes, it is definitely the *calf* muscle. You will have to go off, my dear. There is no way you can continue to play with this injury."
Then Mrs Hiller turned to two of the girls standing nearby and said: "Heather and Tracey, help her to get up and take her back to the changing rooms, please".

Heather and Tracey were actually Susan's best friends and so it was not by chance that they were standing nearby.
"Here, let me!" said a deep voice as her father stepped forward from the crowd, determined to help.
"It's okay, dad. We can manage," said Susan.
It was just too *embarrassing* to let her dad help her off the *pitch* with all her friends standing around and watching.
Mrs Hiller and the girls slowly *helped* Susan *to her feet*. She put her arms around Tracey and Heather, while Heather carried her stick. She then slowly *limped* from the field, trying to put all her weight on her left leg. The crowd from St. Mary's clapped and *cheered*, giving her a hero's reception as she was led off the *pitch*. After a *stern* look from their trainer, some of the Merrywood girls began to clap as well as they watched Susan being helped away. From a distance

a small crowd of boys had also *gathered* to watch.
"Poor Susan," said Arthur. He had *fancied* Susan for a long time, but was too shy to *ask her out*.
"I hope she isn't hurt too bad! It looked really terrible when she crashed to the grass like that!"
"Don't worry," said George, the boy standing next to him. "She will be fine. She is a tough fighter, your Susan!" Arthur's face turned bright red. "What do you mean?" he asked.
"You know just what I mean!" said George in a firm voice. Meanwhile further back in the crowd there was a small group of *guys* who seemed very pleased with what they had seen.
"Serves her right!" said the tall *guy* in the old school blazer. "She's a real little *witch* that girl. She is so *stuck-up*, too."
"Yeah," said another.
"Come one, let's go. This match is boring anyway." Two of the gang *turned on their heels* and *headed back* to the main school exit, unnoticed by the rest of the crowd. In the distance the whistle blew as the hockey match restarted for the final minutes. Mrs Hiller had sent on three *substitutes* to cover for the missing girls. Susan and her friends had finally reached the girls' changing rooms. Heather and Tracey guided Susan to the *bench* where she had hung up all her clothes. She sat down *exhausted*.
"I don't think I can *face* the shower," she said. "I will just have to go home dirty and shower there. Anyway, my parents are waiting outside, so I want to be as quick as possible."

Übung 3: Übersetze die Verben und enträtsele das Lösungswort!

1. halten ☐ _ _ _
2. spielen _ _ ☐ _

3. helfen _ _ _ ☐
4. erscheinen _ ☐ _ _ _ _
5. versuchen _ _ ☐

Lösung: _ _ _ _ _

Heather and Tracey helped Susan into her school uniform. Putting on her socks was the most difficult and they decided to leave one knee sock off, *due to* the pain in her leg.
"Here," said Tracey. "Let me carry your shoe and your sock."
"Thanks!" said Susan. "I don't know what I would do without friends like you!"
Despite the obvious pain she was in, she smiled and looked up at Heather and Tracey, who were standing by to help. She pulled on her school blazer and then felt into the right-hand pocket for her *locket*. At that moment a look of shock and horror came over her face.
"My *locket*!" she cried. "It's gone!"

Chapter 2: Blackmail by Text Message

"Are you sure you had your *locket* with you?" asked Tracey.
"Of course," answered Susan. "I always wear my *locket*, you know that."
"Look in the other pockets," said Heather, trying to sound optimistic. Susan quickly checked through all her pockets, but there was no sign of the missing *locket*. In a state of panic she even picked up the blazer and shook it upside down. All the contents of the pockets fell out. Handkerchiefs, a *comb*, a chocolate bar, several hair bands, some coins, a few old toffees and even some pens fell to the floor, but no *locket*.

"I can't believe it!" she cried. "It's gone! It's gone! It's gone! Someone has been in here and stolen my *locket*."
"Calm down," said Heather. "There has to be an explanation. We have to find out who took it and how to get it back. Hold on, I will just go outside and tell your parents."
"No!" cried Susan. "Don't tell my parents. They mustn't know. They will kill me if they find out I left my *locket* in my blazer in the changing rooms. They are always telling me to take better care of my stuff. If they find out that I left the *locket* in my blazer I will get into big trouble."

Übung 4: Welches Wort ist das „schwarze Schaf"? Unterstreiche das nicht in die Reihe passende Wort!

! ÜBUNG 4

1. breathe, eat, apple, sleep
2. win, stick, ball, goal
3. happy, anger, sad, hopeful
4. cry, tear, sad, left
5. terrible, wonderful, pleased, satisfied
6. tall, fat, short, shoe
7. always, often, never, new

"But your parents are sure to find out," said Heather. "How can you keep this a secret?"
"You must promise me not to tell anyone," said Susan. "We must keep this a secret."
"Okay, I swear," said Heather.
"Me too," said Tracey.
"The *locket* was a present from my grandmother," said Susan. "It is a family *heirloom* and my gran gave it to me before she died."

Heather and Tracey knew the *locket* well because Susan always wore it. The *locket* had a long gold chain and was oval in shape. It opened and had two photos inside, one of Susan's parents and the other of her grandparents. It was Susan's most precious possession and she *was* very *attached to* it.

"I am just so stupid," cried Susan. "Why didn't I put it in the bag with the *valuables* that the coach collected? I have to get it back. Who could have taken it?"

"Don't worry!" said Heather. "We will get it back for you. Maybe someone just took it for a practical joke. I mean they can't really sell it, can they? Not with your photos fixed in it."

"They can always take out the photos," said Susan. "But no, I don't think someone took it for the money. I think someone was trying to *get at* me. It just isn't fair! What have I ever done to hurt anyone?"

ÜBUNG 5 !

Übung 5: Lies weiter und setze die Verben in Klammern ins Simple Past!

With that, she (1. sit) __________ down on the *bench* and (2. cry) __________ again, tears streaming down her cheeks. Heather and Tracey both (3. put) __________ their arms around her shoulders and (4. try) __________ to *comfort* her.

"Don't cry," they (5. say) __________. "We will get it back for you, we promise. Now come on, let's get outside and get you to your parents. They will be wondering what is going on."

"Okay," said Susan, drying her eyes. "But remember, not a word about the *locket*."

"Alright!" said Heather. "Don't worry, we will keep this secret. We won't tell anyone, we promise."

"Yes, you can trust us," said Tracey.

Heather (6. help) __________ Susan put her blazer over her shoulders and the two girls helped her *limp* out of the changing rooms. Her parents (7. be) __________ waiting outside.

Susan's mum and dad came *rushing* across when they saw her coming out.
"Susan, darling!" said her mum. "Are you alright? That was a terrible fall you had."
Susan's mum was always worrying about her and it was *embarrassing* sometimes, but today Susan felt so awful that she just fell into the arms of her mum and wept and wept.
"There, there my love," said her dad, as caring as always. "Let's get you home and put your leg up. Thank goodness it was not broken. That was a great goal you *scored*, well done!"
Susan looked across at her dad and managed a smile. Dear old dad, he was always good at *cheering* her *up*.

Susan said goodbye to her friends. Secretly, she decided to make a plan to get back the *locket* and she was sure that she would need their help.
"Come and see me tomorrow!" she said.
Then her parents helped her into the car and they drove carefully to 12 Featherwood Street. As they arrived Susan was delighted to see their little house. Her dad helped her up into her bedroom and asked if she wanted anything.
"No," said Susan. "I just need some *rest*, thanks."

Übung 6: Beantworte die Fragen zum Text!

1. Which school does Susan go to?

____

2. Who are her best friends?

____

3. What is her father like?

____

4. Who gave Susan the locket?

____

5. What did Mrs Hiller blow?

____

Susan fell into her bed and once her dad had gone she started crying again. What was she going to do? She just couldn't tell them about her *locket*. Would she ever get it back, she wondered? Tracey and Heather would be sure to help. She just had to find a solution.

She lay on the bed and stared at the ceiling. Sleep seemed impossible. Then suddenly she heard a familiar sound. 'Deedle do da da, deedle do da da': her *mobile phone* was ringing. Quickly she rolled over and picked it up from her bedside table.
"You have a message," said the display. She pressed the button and read the words "*r u* missing something?"
What? she thought. Who could this possibly be? She did not know the person sending the message, as her phone said 'Number not

recognized'. Typical, she thought. Someone is just *winding me up*.

Susan loved her *mobile phone*. In fact you could say she was really *addicted to* her phone. She was always *texting* her friends and even slept with the *mobile* by her bedside. Any time of day the phone went she would always jump to answer it. Whenever she heard the ringing tone 'deedle do da da, deedle do da da', she knew she had a message and dropped everything to get to the phone. This time however, it was different. Who was the mystery person who had sent her a message? It must be the person who had taken her *locket*, she thought.

She grabbed the phone, typed in the reply "Who *r u*?" and then pressed the 'Send' button. It seemed like forever as she waited for the reply and then came the sound 'deedle do da da, deedle do da da'. Her fingers were trembling as she pressed the 'Read' button.

"*u r 2 nosy*! Do *u* want *yr locket* back?"

Susan was tempted to scream and shout out:

"Of course I do, you idiot," but she did not want to alarm her parents, so she managed to control her temper, putting her hand over her mouth.

"Of course I do!" she then typed back. "Who *r u*?" she typed in once more, desperate to know who had her precious possession.

"*u* will never know!" came the immediate reply. "Just do as I say or *u* will never *c yr locket* again! Tell *no1*" said the message. "Get us £200 by Friday or *u* will never *c yr locket* again!" wrote the mystery caller.

What? thought Susan. Two hundred pounds? How can I get such a lot of money? I only have 20 *quid* in savings. He was crazy! She was being *blackmailed*.

Susan took a deep breath and thought, calm down, girl, think what to do next. How could she get so much money? Her first thought was to play for more time. "Friday is *2* short notice. I need more time *pls*," she *texted* back.

ÜBUNG 7

*Übung 7: Vervollständige die Sätze mit **my, your, his (2x), her (2x), their** und **our**!*

1. Susan said: "Where is __________ locket?"
2. Heather and Tracey like __________ school.
3. Susan said: "Someone has stolen __________ locket."
4. Susan told me that a thief had stolen __________ locket.
5. Arthur looked at __________ friend.
6. We have lost __________ money.
7. Susan got the locket from __________ gran.
8. Susan's father loves __________ daughter.

But the answer was short and final.

"Get the money by Friday or *u* will never *c yr locket* again! Do not *txt bk* and tell NO-ONE!!!" came back the demand. It was clear that it was impossible to discuss the matter with this person. Then came another short message a few seconds later: "*u* will hear from us again!"

Us, thought Susan. So, was there more than one person? Was there a whole gang in on this? Or was someone trying to *fool* her?

She crashed on the bed and *pounded* the pillows with her *fists*.

"It just isn't fair!" she cried. "It just isn't fair!"

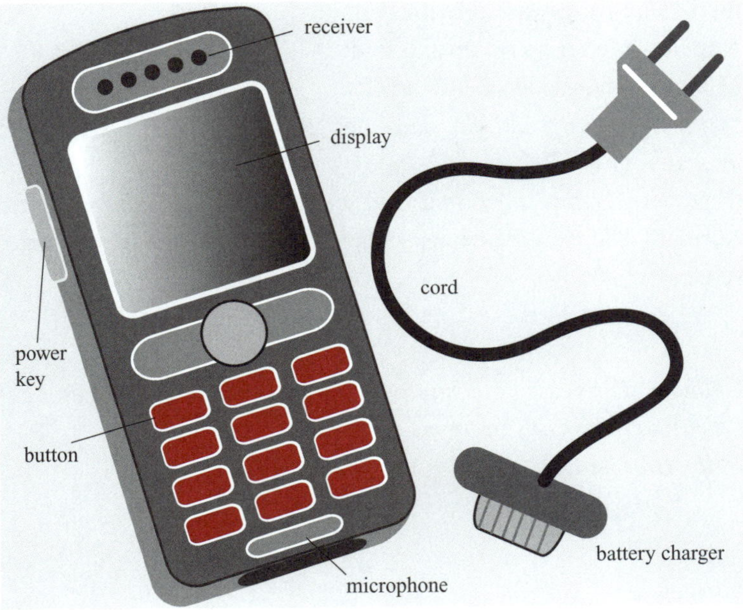

At that moment came a loud knock on the door.
"Are you alright, dear?" came the caring voice of her mother.
In her desperation she had forgotten all about being calm. Quickly she *rubbed* her eyes and blew her nose.
"Can I come in?" asked her mother, sounding rather anxious.
"Yes, just a minute, mum," came the reply.
Susan put her *mobile* in the *drawer* of the *bedside cabinet* and closed it before shouting:
"Okay, you can come in now."
The door opened and her mum entered the room.
"Oh my poor dear," she said with a soft voice. "Have you been crying?"
For the second time that day Susan *flung* her arms around her mum and *sobbed* her heart out. It was all just too stressful. She was grate-

ful that her mum was there for her.
After a while Susan sat up and said:
“Thanks, mum. That’s better now.”
“That was quite a fall you had,” her mum said. “Can I just take a look at your leg?”
Obediently Susan rolled over and let her mother examine her leg. Normally she would have resisted, but today she was happy to get some sympathy.

ÜBUNG 8

Übung 8: Ordne den Substantiven die folgenden Verben richtig zu! Verwende jedes Verb zweimal.
(falls, runs, sings)

1. The rain ____________
2. The bird ____________
3. The rabbit ____________
4. The train ____________
5. The apple ____________
6. The girl ____________

“I think we will have to take you to the doctor’s with this,” her mother said.
“No, it’s okay, mum. I’ll be fine, and anyway it’s Friday and the doctor’s will be closed. I definitely don’t need to go to hospital either, it’s not that bad.”
“Well, if you’re sure. I will just quickly get some *ointment* and *rub* it *in*.”
Susan allowed her mum to *rub in* the *ointment* and then said:

“Thanks, mum, but I need a bit of *space* now. I just need to *chill* for a while. Could you leave me alone, please?”
In fact she could not wait to *text* her friends the news of the *blackmail*, but there was no way she would tell her mum. The message had said ‘tell NO-ONE’ but she knew she could trust Heather and Tracey.
As soon as her mum was gone she opened the *drawer* of her *bedside cabinet* and took out her phone. She had to talk to Tracey to tell her the news. At first she wanted to ring her, but then she *hesitated*. What if her parents overheard her? It was just too risky to call and so she decided to *text* her instead. She knew that her parents would not let her out of the house today. There was no school tomorrow, so she decided to meet Tracey in the park nearby.

Übung 9: Bilde Sätze mit dem Komparativ!

1. June/January (hot)

June is hotter than January.

2. running/walking (fast)

3. Russian/English (difficult)

4. hockey stick/tennis racquet (long)

5. house/flat (big)

6. grandmother/mother (old)

The girls spent a lot of time *hanging out* in the park. It was one of the few places they could meet without being disturbed by grown-ups. Susan quickly typed in the message.

"I need *yr* help. Meet me in the park *2moro @* 9," it said, then she pressed the 'Send' button and scrolled down the menu until she got to the name Tracey in her address book. Then she thought again. She would need a lot of help and she decided to *text* Heather as well. It was a good idea to get her involved as well and she was at the changing rooms when the *theft* of the *locket* was discovered. Tracey was really her best friend, but she could trust Heather as well. After she had sent the second message she sat back on the bed *racking her brains*.

Who could have taken the *locket*? It must be someone who knew her well enough to get hold of her *mobile* number. Was it someone on the hockey team? There were one or two girls who did not like her. Amanda Jones had been really *nasty* to her since she had started *going out with* Giles. She *claimed* that Susan had stolen Giles from her, because Amanda and Giles had been *going out* together for six months, but later Giles had *split up* with Amanda shortly before he met Susan. And there was also Beverly Little who could not stand the sight of her. Beverly was jealous of Susan and Susan was *convinced* that this was because she attracted boys easily and Beverly had never had a boyfriend, as far as Susan knew. Well, was that her fault?

Susan looked in the mirror at her long blonde hair. Yes, many boys did find her attractive, but she could not help her good looks and that was no reason for Beverly to be so *nasty* to her.

Yes, maybe Beverly could have taken the *locket*, she thought.

Then she remembered that Amanda and Beverly had been on the *substitutes' bench*. They could easily have slipped into the changing rooms to get the *locket* while no-one was looking. Maybe they had planned this before the game?

Übung 10: Wähle das passende Wort für jeden Satz aus und unterstreiche es!

! ÜBUNG 10

1. Susan hit/hurt her leg.
2. Arthur means/thinks Susan is very attractive.
3. The handy/mobile was ringing.
4. She cleaned/blew her nose.
5. Tracey looked/watched in the mirror.
6. It was too much/many money.

Susan used to be friends with Amanda before she had started *dating* Giles, and so she would still have her *mobile* number as well. It had to be someone who knew she always wore the *locket* and how much it meant to her. Then in a flash another idea came to her. Perhaps it was Giles, her ex-boyfriend? He had been really horrible to her when they had *split up*. He also swore that he would get his revenge. Yes, suddenly she was certain it was him. She decided she was going to make him pay for what he had done. Her first thought was to call him right away and ask him to tell her the truth, but she thought he would be sure to *deny* it over the phone.

Then at that moment she received a text message on her *mobile*. Tracey confirmed that she would be at the park tomorrow, and shortly afterwards Heather responded, too, saying she would also be there.

It was now 10 p.m. and Susan realized just how *exhausted* she was.

ÜBUNG 11 !

Übung 11: Lies weiter und ordne die Buchstaben zu einem sinnvollen Wort!

After the hockey (1. hamtc) ______________, the accident and then the *blackmail* shock she had lost all sense of time. She *yawned* and then stretched her (2. mars) ______________ high. I should try to get some sleep, she thought. After much struggling she managed to get into her pyjamas. Again she did not (3. anwt) ______________ to ask for help and *despite* her sore (4. gle) ______________ she managed to get ready for bed, *crawled* (5. derun) ______________ her *duvet* and then switched off the bedside light. A few minutes later came a knock at the (6. rood) ______________.

"Are you okay? Can I (7. meco) ______________ in?" asked her mum.

"Yes, mum," (8. aisd) ______________ Susan.

Normally Susan could be very *grumpy* and she often drove her parents crazy, but after the shock things were different. There was no way she wanted to tell her mum what was going on. But her mum just quickly wished her a good night and left the room again.

The next morning Susan woke early. She looked over at the electric alarm clock, which said 5:30 a.m. She could not believe that it was so early. Usually she woke up at around 7 a.m., but last night she had slept very badly and had had a nightmare with dark figures reaching around her neck.

The loss of her *locket* had shaken her badly and she had no idea how she was going to *raise* so much money. Two hundred pounds was a huge sum. She rolled over and tried to go back to sleep, but the thoughts kept going round in her mind. Yesterday she thought that Giles had taken her *locket*, but now she wasn't so sure any more. Would he really have *crept* into the changing rooms and gone through her things? Did he hate her so much? She had *been* very *fond of* Giles and had *dated* him for over eight months, but the *break-up* had been hard for him.
Towards the end of their relationship they had nothing to talk about any more and she just could not *cope with* the long silences.

Übung 12: Ordne jedem Wortanfang den passenden zweiten Teil zu und trage die richtige Nummer in das Kästchen ein!

ÜBUNG 12 !

1. ☐ changing	a) mother
2. ☐ black	b) hear
3. ☐ heir	c) room
4. ☐ goal	d) mail
5. ☐ grand	e) keeper
6. ☐ over	f) loom

At around 8:45 a.m. Susan *limped* downstairs to find her dad reading the paper and her mum busy hoovering the lounge. She had arranged to meet Tracey and Heather in the park at 9 a.m. and knew it would take her a bit longer than usual to get there.
"My leg is much better now, mum," she said. Normally she hated lying, but this was an emergency. "Look, I can walk on it well." She *clenched her teeth together* and was able to walk on her leg across the lounge without showing any pain.

"Well, if you're really sure," said her mum.

"Be careful," said her dad. "I don't want you to have any more accidents."

"Okay," said Susan. "I will be really careful, I promise. You don't need to worry."

She moved slowly and carefully to the front door. Once she had closed it behind her, she breathed a sigh of *relief*.

ÜBUNG 13 !

Übung 13: Welche der Erklärungen stimmt? Kreuze die richtige Antwort an!

1. She was determined to reach the goal.
   a) ☐ She was very short.
   b) ☐ She wanted to score a goal.
   c) ☐ She put out her arms to touch the goal.

2. She tried to fight off tears.
   a) ☐ She punched someone with her fists.
   b) ☐ She tried not to cry.
   c) ☐ She was very afraid.

3. Susan was attached to her locket.
   a) ☐ It was tied around her neck.
   b) ☐ She could not let go of it.
   c) ☐ She liked it very much.

4. Her dad cheered her up.
   a) ☐ He made her feel better.
   b) ☐ He shouted hooray.
   c) ☐ He told her she was pretty.

5. She racked her brains.
   a) ☐ She asked for help.
   b) ☐ She scratched her head.
   c) ☐ She thought it over.

The park was roughly five minutes' walk away, but today it took much longer *due to* Susan's bad leg. She entered the park through the main gate and could see her two friends Heather and Tracey waiting for her at their usual meeting spot over by the *swings*. When they saw her they both got up from the park *bench* where they had been waiting and ran towards her.

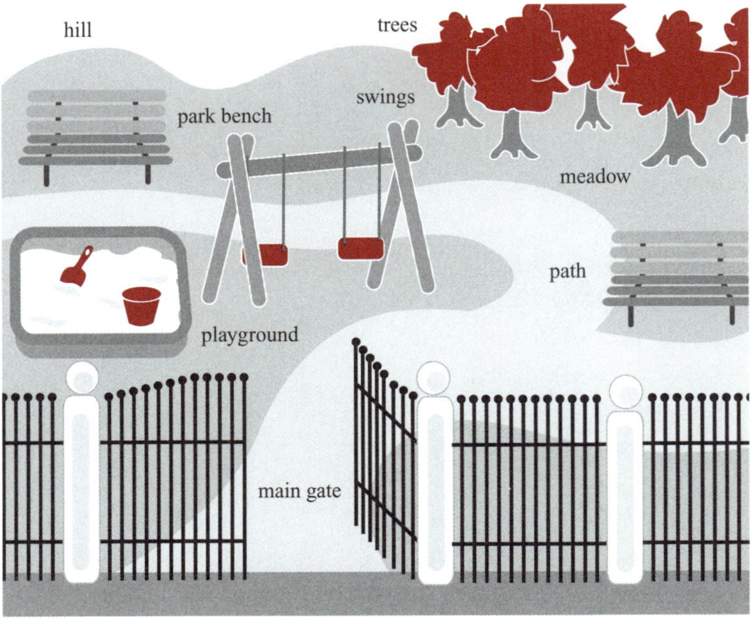

"Hey Susan!" yelled Tracey. "Great to see you! I was really worried about you yesterday. *What's up?*"

"Yes, you must tell us everything!" said Heather. "We are dying to know what is going on."

"Well," began Susan. "Just after I got home last night I got this, you see. Some *jerk* has stolen my *locket* and wants me to pay him or her two hundred pounds to hand it back! I mean – can you believe it? Two hundred *quid* just to get back my *locket*!"

"Do you have any idea who it could be?" asked Heather, anxious to know the identity of the thief.

"The message said 'Number not recognized'. I tried to *text* back and get the sender to give his or her name, but of course they did not want to, did they?"

"Yes, I guess a *blackmailer* would be really stupid to tell you their name," said Tracey.

ÜBUNG 14 !

Übung 14: Sind die folgenden Aussagen richtig? Markiere mit richtig ✔ oder falsch – !

1. Susan missed the goal. ☐
2. Hot water eases pain. ☐
3. Arthur fancies Susan. ☐
4. Giles was blackmailed. ☐
5. Susan's father is reading. ☐
6. Giles is Susan's boyfriend. ☐
7. Susan was often grumpy. ☐

"You must have some idea who has taken the *locket*," continued Heather. "I mean – who would want to steal from you? It must be someone who knows what that *locket* means to you and someone who has got access to your *mobile phone* number. So it must be someone you know."

"Well, I do have a few ideas," said Susan. "First I thought of Amanda Jones. I mean, she has been really *mad* at me since I started *going out with* Giles. And then of course there is Beverly Little who has never really liked me and is always making *nasty* remarks. Both of them were not playing in the team on Friday, so they could easily have gone back to the changing rooms without being noticed by anyone.

Maybe they even did it together. Of course it could possibly have been Giles. He has been so *mad* at me ever since we *split up*."

"What?" said Tracey. "Do you really think Giles would do this to you? Was he that *mad*?"

"We have to treat him as the *prime suspect*," said Susan.

"Is there anyone else who comes to mind?" asked Heather. "I mean, you really seem to have a lot of enemies!"

"It's not my fault!" cried Susan. "I always try to be nice to people, it's just that some people don't appreciate how hard I try. I really do!"

At this point Susan looked as if she was about to cry, so Tracey quickly stepped in to calm her down:

"Hey, keep cool, just relax," said Tracey. "Don't get *upset* again, that won't help at all. Here, have a tissue and dry your eyes."

"Yeah, sorry," said Heather. "I didn't mean to *get at* you. I just was a bit surprised that there are so many people, who *are*, shall we say, *out to get* you."

"Okay," said Tracey. "Let's get down to business. We have three possible suspects. How are we going to find out who took the *locket* and what are we going to do about the money? I mean two hundred *quid* is a lot of cash to *raise*."

Heather looked at Tracey.

"Maybe we should get some help with this," said Heather. "I mean, have you thought about contacting the police?"

ÜBUNG 15 !

Übung 15: Lies weiter und setze die richtigen Präpositionen ein! ***(for, to, out)***

"No!" replied Susan. "There's no way can we contact them. The message said 'tell no-one' and my parents are sure (1.) ________ find (2.) ________ if we contact the police. I trust you two, but we can't tell anyone else. We have (3.) ________ solve this ourselves. If the thief finds (4.) ________ we have told anyone the *locket* may be gone (5.) ________ ever. I'm sure he or she would just *dump* it somewhere and that would be the last I would see of it. I just can't *take* that *risk*. That *locket* really means a lot (6.) ________ me!"

"We will have to look (7.) ________ the *locket* ourselves," agreed Tracey.

"Alright, alright," said Heather. "We won't go to the police and we won't tell anyone. Do you agree, Tracey?"

"That's cool with me!" said Tracey.

"Well, let's work out a plan of action then," said Heather.

Heather turned to Susan and said:

"Well, Susan, let's look at this logically. Who is your *prime suspect*? Who do you think is most likely to have taken the *locket*?"

"I really can't say," said Susan. "As I told you, Giles, Amanda or Beverly could all have taken it, or somebody else. I am really not sure who it was."

"Well," said Heather, "we have to start investigating each suspect then. Who do we start with?"

"I only see Amanda or Beverly at school and so we can't *check on* them until Monday."
"Okay," said Heather. "Let's start with Giles then. Where does he normally *hang out* on Saturday mornings?"
"That's easy," said Susan. "He's always over at the shopping centre on Derby Road with his little gang. They always *hang out* at the billiard café there. But I really don't know if I can *face* him alone. I mean, I haven't spoken to him since we *split up* six months ago."
"Keep cool," said Heather. "We will be with you all the way!"
"Yeah, that's what friends are for!" continued Tracey.
"Thanks, girls," said Susan, *giving* them both *a* quick *hug*. "I don't know what I would do without you two!"
The three girls then made their way towards the shopping centre on Derby Road. It was a brand new shopping centre with three floors. In the girls' opinion it was the best thing that had happened to Middlesex for ages. It had *loads of* trendy outlet stores selling clothes, fashion jewellery and music. Normally the three girls loved going there and trying on the latest fashions, but today was different. Today they had a mission.

Übung 16: Beantworte die Fragen zum Text!

1. Where did Susan keep her mobile?

....

2. Why did the three girls go to the shopping centre?

....

3. What did Susan do with her pillows?

....

4. What did Susan's mum rub on her leg?

5. What colour is Susan's hair?

6. Did Giles finish with Susan?

Chapter 3: Showdown at the Shopping Centre

The shopping centre was just a short bus ride away. They often walked, but because of Susan's sore leg the girls decided to catch the bus. They entered the centre on the ground floor and wandered around for a short time.

"Normally Giles and his gang always *hang out* in the billiard café on the top floor," said Susan. "Let's see if he and his friends are here today."

The three friends went up the escalators to the top floor of the centre and slowly made their way to the billiard café at the end of the row of shops. As they got closer, Susan started to realize just how nervous she was about *facing* Giles. When they had *split up* she had been very *bold* and just told him that she did not want to *go out with* him anymore. However, she had not anticipated his reaction. He was furious, had called her a stupid *stuck-up* cow and marched away.

Since that day Susan had always *avoided* him. She had seen him around, but had not spoken one word to him. For a long time she had told herself she was 'over him'. However, now that she was about to speak to him face to face, she realized just how nervous she was. In fact she felt herself shaking a bit as she thought of meeting him again. She told herself it was probably just the shock of the accident yesterday, but when she got within sight of the door of the café she panicked and turned around, quickly walking in the other direction.

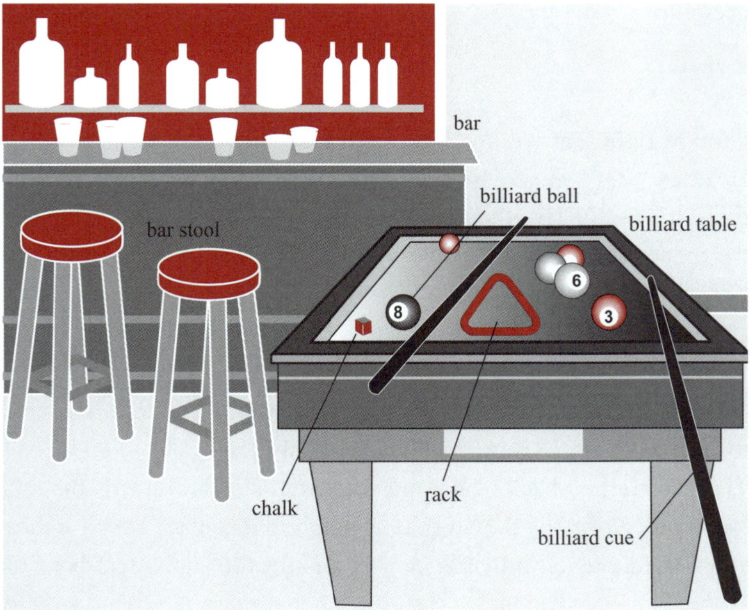

Übung 17: Lies weiter und setze das passende Wort ein!
(time, locket, feet, explode, thing)

"Hey Susan!" Tracey grabbed her arm and came alongside her. "*What's up?*"

"I just…, I'm just not sure if this is the right (1.) ____________ to do," said Susan, trying to sound convincing.

"Have you got cold (2.) ______________?" asked Heather.

"No, no," replied Susan, playing for (3.) ______________. "It's just that I'm worried what he might do if I confront him face to face. I mean, he might (4.) __________________ and go for me. He might even throw away the (5.) ____________________ and I would never see it again."

"You're right that we don't know exactly how he will react," said Heather. "But I'm sure he won't get rid of the *locket* that quickly. I think if he's after two hundred *quid* then he will want to wait to get the money."
"That's true," replied Susan. She was slowly trying to pluck up courage to *face* him again and did not want to show her fear to her friends.
"Okay!" she said finally, taking a deep breath. "Let's do it. We have to find out if it was him and this is the only way."
The girls turned back again and wandered slowly towards the billiard café. Normally they would never go in this place because they considered playing billiards *daft.* It was for the adolescent boys or '*yobs'* as they called them. The girls much preferred looking around the shops for trendy clothes, but this was the only way to get to Giles.
They entered the door and slowly moved among the tables looking for Giles. Suddenly Heather pulled Susan's arm.
"Look, there he is! Over there by the corner table!" she said.
"Where?" replied Susan. She looked over to where Heather was pointing, but she didn't see him.
"Behind the big *guy* with the black leather jacket," said Heather.
"Oh! I see him now," said Susan.

Susan knew the *guy* in the leather jacket only too well. It was Adrian Cholerton. He was Giles's best *mate* and the two went everywhere together. Susan had never liked him and he *gave* her *the creeps*. But now was not the time for hesitation. Susan turned to her friends and said:
"Come on, girls, let's make our move."

Übung 18: Lies weiter und setze das Gegenteil der Wörter in Klammern ein!

ÜBUNG 18 !

The three girls walked (1. quickly) s__________ between the billiard tables towards Giles and his *mates*. He was actually with Adrian and two other *guys* who Susan knew by sight, but she did not know their names.

Susan had really hoped that Giles would be alone, but now it would be (2. easy) d__________ with all his *mates* around him. Nevertheless she was determined to approach him. As she moved (3. further) c__________ to the table where he was standing, Adrian stopped in the middle of his shot and looked up. Instantly he recognized the (4. big) s__________ gang of girls and his eyes *narrowed*.

"Oh, look who we have here!" said Adrian in a sarcastic voice. "If it isn't Goldilocks and her two bears!" he continued, referring to Susan's (5. short) l__________ blonde hair.

Just a short distance behind him, Giles looked up and his eyes met Susan's. For a moment Susan thought she saw a look of compassion on his face. Perhaps he still felt something for her after all. Perhaps she was wrong in suspecting him and he had nothing to do with this whole business.

She just had to find out. She had to be sure if he had stolen the *locket* or not.

"Someone to see you, I think," continued Adrian. He stood aside to let Susan approach Giles. This was exactly what she had wanted to *avoid*, a *showdown* in public, with all his *mates* standing around. She opened her mouth to speak.

"Giles, I just, I just wanted to know…"

Übung 19: Lies weiter und setze die Verben in der richtigen Zeitform ein!

"What!" snapped Giles back quickly. "Have you come to *ask me out* again?"

His friends (1. laugh) ______________; he (2. be) ______________ feeling really strong now. Since Susan had finished with him he had been very miserable and now he (3. feel) ______________ his anger *rising up*.

"Yeah – you tell her!" joined in one of the other boys standing nearby.

"Got something on your mind?" (4. continue) ______________ Giles in an abrupt tone.

“I (5. be) ______________ just wondering if you…”

Susan could not finish her sentence before Giles interrupted:

“If I what? If I want to *go out with* you again? You *have a nerve*, coming here and *crawling* back to me after how you treated me!”

The blood (6. rise) ________________ to Susan’s cheeks and she struggled to speak. She had (7. lose) ______________ her nerve.

Smelling fear the other boys turned on her quickly:
“*What’s up?* Lost your tongue now, have you? Is Goldilocks going to cry now, is she?” they *piled on the pressure*.
“Just leave her alone!” shouted Tracey, trying to defend her friend and to show the boys that they were not going to be *bullied*. She realized it was useless to ask about the *locket* now. They had really *blown* it.
The tears were now streaming down Susan’s cheeks. She did not know if it was the pain of rejection or the shooting pain in her leg that hurt the most. She just wanted to get out of this place as soon as possible. She felt *humiliated*. How stupid she had been confronting Giles on his home territory!

Übung 20: Setze die richtigen Präpositionen ein!

In front (1.) __________ his gang Giles was playing the strong man role, but secretly he *was* still *sweet on* Susan. His *pride* had been hurt when she had finished with him though and he certainly was not going (2.) __________ admit to his friends that he still *had a soft spot for* her.

Meanwhile Susan had now made it (3.) __________ of the café with Tracey and Heather (4.) __________ either side of her. She did not look back. She definitely did not want the *guys* to see that she had been crying.

“Come on,” said Tracey. “Let’s get you home. *No point in* getting *upset* (5.) __________ those losers.”

“Yeah,” said Heather. “Nothing more we can do here. There is no way they are going to talk to us now.”
“Sorry,” said Susan. “I really messed that up, didn’t I?”
“We have to *trap* them somehow,” said Heather.
“Yes, but how?” asked Tracey.
“There must be someone else who we could get them to talk to,” said Heather.
“Look, girls,” said Susan. “I’ve really had enough now, I’m *done in*. Can’t we leave it for now and get on home? It’s almost lunchtime and my parents will wonder where I have been if I get back too late.”
“Alright,” said Tracey. “Let’s get you home and perhaps we can meet again after lunch.”
The girls went back down the escalators towards the main exit of the shopping centre.
Down below two young boys had been *hanging around* outside the ice cream stand. They had a good view of the top floor of the shopping centre and had seen Susan and her friends come out of the café in a hurry and travel down the escalators. They were the same boys who had seen Susan get injured during the hockey match. George and Arthur were both members of the chess club, where Susan

played as well. Arthur had *fancied* Susan for a long time. When he saw her coming out of the café with her two friends he realized that something must be going on, because Susan and her friends never went near the billiard café normally.
Arthur plucked up courage. This was his chance to make a move.

Übung 21: Trage die fehlenden Buchstaben in die Lücken ein!

1. A part of the school uniform is a b _ _ z _ _.
2. A replacement player is a s _ b _ _ it _ _ e.
3. Another word for 'very tired' is e _ h _ _ _ _ e _.
4. Something of value is something p _ _ ci _ _ _.
5. When you are very worried you are a _ _ i _ _ _.
6. When you break up with someone you s _ li _ up.
7. When you are tired you _ aw _.

He stepped out from behind the ice cream stand just as Susan, Heather and Tracey came down the escalator.
"Hi, Susan!" he said, his heart *pounding* as he spoke. Then he saw her red eyes and noticed she had obviously been crying. It was too late to stop now.
"Are you alright?" he continued. He felt stupid saying that, but the words just slipped out before he could stop himself. As soon as he had spoken he felt the blood *rush* to his cheeks.
However, before he had a chance to continue, Heather stepped in: "Sorry, Arthur, we have to leave, we don't have time to stop and chat. Excuse us please."

And with that the girls disappeared out of the main door, leaving Arthur and George standing.

"What was that all about?" asked George.

"I don't know," replied Arthur. "But I am going to find out. Come on, let's go up to the café and see who's in there. Susan was crying when she came out, so somebody must have been pretty *mean* to her. I have a good idea who it was, but let's go and make sure."

The two boys ran up the escalators and then made their way to the café. They had often been there, so it did not look *suspicious* when they went inside. Casually they walked over to the bar and ordered two cokes. They sat and drank them while looking around to see who was in.

ÜBUNG 22 !

Übung 22: Welche Gegenteile gehören zusammen? Ordne zu!

1. ☐ tall	a) happy
2. ☐ first	b) down
3. ☐ further	c) nearer
4. ☐ up	d) short
5. ☐ quickly	e) last
6. ☐ sad	f) slowly

Sure enough, over in the corner were Giles and Adrian, together with two other *lads* who they did not know. They were happily playing billiards and seemed very pleased with themselves. Arthur tried to get a bit closer so that he could hear what they were saying. He wanted to find out if they were talking about Susan.

He got an angry look from Adrian as he got closer. One of those looks that said: "Don't even think about speaking to me".

Arthur and George quickly they finished their cokes and left.

"Well, what do you make of that?" said Arthur. "Do you think they could have been *bothering* Susan?"
"I don't see who else it could have been," said George. "There was no-one else in the place that I recognized."
"But what was Susan doing there?" said Arthur with a puzzled look on his face. "I mean, she finished with Giles ages ago. They never even speak to each other normally."
"Well, she certainly wanted something from him today," said George.
"And it was obviously something she did not get!" replied Arthur. "I simply must find out what is going on."
"Not today, you won't," answered George. "You saw the look Heather gave you. I would leave it until you see her at school next week."
Reluctantly Arthur agreed. He was burning to know what was going on and hoped that in some way he could *find favour with* Susan. He *had* a really big *crush on* her and wanted to help her.
Meanwhile Susan, Tracey and Heather had reached the bus stop to catch the bus back home. They sat downstairs as Susan's leg was hurting badly now and they did not want to put her through any more pain.

Übung 23: Lies weiter und unterstreiche die sechs Wörter, die falsch geschrieben sind. Verbessere sie anschließend!

! ÜBUNG 23

When Susan got home her dad was waiting for her.
"I thaught I told you to take it easy," said her dad, sounding very *cross*. "Yesterday you could hardly walk *due to* the pain and today you are runing around all over the place."
"I'm fin, dad, really. You don't need to worry."

In reality she was feeling really *lousy*, but she did not want her parents to kno this. They were certain to make her stay in if they knew how she really felt. Her dad was always easier to *fool* than her mum. She had got very good at *twisting* him *around her little finger*. She looked her dad straight in the eyes and said in a soft voice:
"I really am fine, my leg is a lot better now."
Her dad looked at her *suspiciously*, not shure if she was pretending to be well and trying to *fool* him. He *hesitated* before answering:
"Well, I want you to stay in for the rest of the day and that is final!"
Susan realized that this tim he meant what he said and there would be no way to persuade him to let her go out again.

1. ______________________

2. ______________________

3. ______________________

4. ______________________

5. ______________________

6. ______________________

Susan sighed and went up to her room. A short while later she suddenly heard the ringing tone of her *mobile*. It made her jump. She sat up on the edge of the bed.
"You have a message," said the words in the display. Quickly she pressed the button marked 'Read'.
"I said tell *no1*! Do *u want 2* lose the *locket*?"
Susan stared at the phone, totally shocked. How had they found out that she had spoken to someone? It must have been Giles after all, she thought! She must have really shaken him by approaching him in the shopping centre like that. Now she was certain it was him and she would get revenge for sure. Quickly she dried her red eyes and blew her nose.
Now what should she write back? She was sure of herself now and in the mood for revenge. How could Giles be so *mean*?

Übung 24: Setze die Aussagen ins Simple Past!

1. The team beats us every time. ______________________
2. The sun shines. ______________________
3. He is suspicious. ______________________
4. They are annoyed. ______________________
5. He comes to the park every week. ______________________
6. We have a message. ______________________
7. They win the match. ______________________

She typed a reply message into her phone:
"I told nobody," she wrote. Then she thought for a moment. Was it a good idea to *deny* having told anybody? Surely the *blackmailer* must have seen her talking to somebody about the *locket*? But then she had not even mentioned the *locket* when she approached Giles. How could he have known that she had spoken to anyone? Unless he had just assumed by her reaction that she was planning a counter attack with her friends.
She pressed the 'Delete' key and decided to write a new message. It would be better to admit that she had asked for help and that she needed help to *raise* the money. That would be more likely to keep the *blackmailer* from getting angry. She typed in the new message: "I need help *2* get the money," she wrote, hoping that this would calm the person sending the message.
She waited anxiously for the reply. When it finally came the text read:
"no more chances. Do as I say or *u* will never *c yr locket* again! – Get me £200 *b4* Friday."

Well, that was clear. She wondered if she should answer, but decided to keep the reply short. She did not want to annoy the caller: "Ok, I promise," she typed and pressed the 'Send' button.

! ÜBUNG 25

Übung 25: Lies weiter und setze die Verben ins Simple Past!

She (1. sit) ____________ quietly for a while and (2. think) ____________ about the message. In future she had to be more careful about who she (3. speak) ____________ to. After a while she remembered that she had promised to *text* Heather and Tracey. After the shock of the last message she could not wait to tell her friends. "can *u* come *2* my house now?" she typed in and (4. send) ____________ the text to Tracey.

"sorry, not til 3," (5. come) ____________ back the reply.

"ok, *c u l8r @* 3," she typed back.

Susan then *texted* Heather to get her over as well. But the reply came back:

"sorry, i can't come *2day*. have to go *2* shops with mum."

What! thought Susan. Just when I need her she has to go shopping! Angrily she (6. grab) ____________ her *mobile* and typed in the reply.

"I need *u* here! Can't *yr* mum shop alone?"
"Sorry, I promised her. Will *c u 2moro*!" came the answer.

“Oh shit!” screamed Susan, crashing onto her bed. “This is so unfair.” She punched the bed with her *fists*. What was she to do until three o’clock? Then she remembered the money. Two hundred *quid*, how could she get that much money by Friday? She opened her desk and took out her post office *savings book*. Seventy-five pounds and fifteen pence. Well, that was a nice surprise! She had a lot more money than she thought she had. Maybe she would be able to get the two hundred pounds after all, but then did she want to just hand over the cash without first trying to catch the *blackmailer*? It was all very risky. She lay on the bed and tried to sleep. The clock seemed to go around very slowly, but after a while she was awakened by a knock on the door.
“Susan, are you asleep? There’s someone here to see you, it’s Tracey,” said her mum.
“Okay, I’m coming!” answered Susan. She got up and straightened her dress. When she opened the door Tracey was already standing outside and waiting.
“Hi Tracey!” said Susan. “Good to see you, come on in. Unfortunately, Heather can’t come.”
Tracey came into the bedroom and Susan closed the door behind her. She pressed it hard to make sure it was shut *tight* and no-one could hear them from outside.
“So,” said Tracey. “*What’s up?*”

*Übung 26: Vervollständige die Sätze mit **a, an** oder **the**!*

1. Susan is ______ hockey player.
2. ______ apple is a fruit.
3. She wants to score ______ goal.

4. The girls helped her off ______ field.

5. It was ______ sad day for Susan.

6. Mrs Hiller pressed gently on ______ calf muscle.

7. Susan had ______ excellent eye for the ball.

8. Susan closed ______ door behind her.

9. She has to get ______ money by Friday.

Susan explained how she had received another text message from the *blackmailer* and that she was sure it was Giles. Tracey was of a different opinion.

"Why would Giles *text* you so soon after you confronted him?" she asked. "It just doesn't make sense. If he did have the *locket* he would not want to *arouse suspicion* by contacting you again so soon after your meeting."

Susan had to agree that Tracey *had a point*. Maybe it was not Giles after all. Surely he would not be so stupid as to *text* her and complain that she had told someone about the *locket*. Then she would know for sure it was him who took it.

"But it must have been somebody who knows that you and Heather are helping me find the *locket*," said Susan. "There must be someone who saw us together in the shopping centre and who suspects we were trying to find the *locket*. Who else did we see in there? Can you remember?"

"It was pretty busy," said Tracey. "Lots of people could have seen us. It is easy to follow someone in that place."

She paused, and then suddenly she shouted, "of course, Arthur! He was *hanging around* with that boy George. Maybe the two of them did this as a practical joke to get your attention. You know he has been *chasing* you for ages!"

Chapter 4: The Secret Admirer

On Sunday morning Susan awoke at around 9 a.m. She felt much better after her long sleep. As soon as she got out of bed, she pulled back the curtains and saw that the sun was shining. Well, thank goodness it's stopped raining, she thought. It seemed to have been raining for days. She bent down and examined her leg. The swelling had gone down a lot. It was badly *bruised* and still stiff, but it did not hurt as much as before. When she got up, she saw that the bathroom was free and she decided to have a long bath. She called downstairs:

"I'm just running a bath, okay?"

There was no answer from below, so she went to the top of the stairs and shouted again:

"Mum, dad… I'm having a bath, is that okay?"

Finally her mother's voice answered from below:

"Yes, dear, that's fine. How are you feeling today?"

"Good, thanks. I just need to relax a little."

Normally, whenever she ran a bath somebody decided they needed to use the toilet. It was a real *nuisance* that they only had one toilet in the house. She often wished her parents were rich like Tracey's. Tracey had her own bathroom and toilet. Her house had four bedrooms and they had three bathrooms, one for her parents and even one just for guests. It was just not fair that Susan's parents were poor. Her dad worked in the post office as a chief inspector, while Tracey's dad was some manager of an oil company or something. At Christmas time Tracey always got *loads of* presents and for her birthday too. Susan *was* often *fed up* of being in a middle-class family and dreamed of living a life of luxury like Tracey. Her other friend Heather was more 'normal' however. She was *better-off* than Susan, but her family was not as wealthy as Tracey's.

ÜBUNG 27 !

Übung 27: In den folgenden Sätzen sind die Wörter durcheinander geraten. Bringe sie in die richtige Reihenfolge und beachte dabei die Satzzeichen und Groß- und Kleinschreibung!

1. arms of she her mum fell into the

She fell into the arms of her mum.

2. by mobile her was bedside the

3. in you can come now

4. message the sent who

5. of now space need bit I a

6. anyone tell not do

7. was she get annoyed starting to

Also, Heather was very *down-to-earth* and practical. Sometimes Tracey could be quite a *snob* and she really *got on* Susan's *nerves*. Still, they had been friends ever since they started school at St. Mary's and all three of them were in Year 10 together. Next year they would be taking their *GCSEs* so they had to do a lot of revision. Tracey was very clever at maths (one of Susan's worst subjects), while Susan was much better at French. Heather was more interested in art and spent most of her free time painting or making models out of *clay*. Apart from schoolwork and hockey, Susan also played chess, but found it quite difficult. She was on the chess team at school and they played every Wednesday afternoon. When she thought of chess she remembered Arthur. Tracey had said he had been *chasing* her for ages.

Arthur was a tall *lad* with brown curly hair. He wore glasses and Susan had always thought of him as a bit of a *swot*. He was only in Year 9, but because he was very good at chess, he played on the same team as her. Of course she had noticed that he often seemed to be *hanging around* when she was playing chess, but he had never really spoken much to Susan. He was always talking and trying to be funny with the other players. He liked trying to attract attention to himself. There was no way she would even consider *going out with* someone in Year 9 and he was really not her type at all. Really she had tried to ignore him, but when Tracey said he had been *chasing* her, it rung a bell for Susan. Did Arthur really think he had a chance with her? Could he really have taken her *locket*? Susan found that hard to believe, but it seemed very *suspicious* that he had been *hanging around* in the shopping centre and just happened to be there when she was walking out. What if he had planned the whole thing with that friend of his? What was his name again? George, that was it. Maybe the two of them had planned this together to attract Susan's attention.

ÜBUNG 28 !

Übung 28: Was gehört zusammen? Ordne zu!

1. ☐	to ring	a) a bus
2. ☐	to catch	b) a text message

3. ☐	to find	c) a job
4. ☐	to send	d) a bell
5. ☐	to score	e) a game
6. ☐	to play	f) a goal
7. ☐	to answer	g) a book
8. ☐	to run	h) a question
9. ☐	to read	i) a bath

Perhaps they had intended to *put the blame on* Giles and his friends. Then when the *locket* turned up again they could claim to be heroes for *recovering* the stolen *locket*! It was a complicated theory, but it was possible that Arthur could have planned this whole thing just to win over Susan. How stupid some boys could be!

Susan was used to boys *chasing* her at school. Her long blonde hair and her good figure meant that she found it easy to attract them. However, the idea that some boy could steal her property and then try to *put the blame on* her ex-boyfriend Giles made Susan really *mad*.

She decided that she would march up to Arthur at school tomorrow and tell him she had uncovered his plan. Maybe she should *text* him now and tell him to bring back her *locket* at once.

The sound of running water interrupted Susan's daydreaming. The bath was running over and she *rushed* to turn off the water. The bathroom floor was flooded with water and it took her a while and a number of towels to mop it all up. She would have to be more careful next time.

For a long time she lay in the bath enjoying the feeling of the warm water and lots of bubbles. It was a great way to relax. Normally nothing much happened on Sundays in the Wilson household. If there was no hockey match to play, Susan often found the day quite boring, but today she was happy just to have a *rest*.

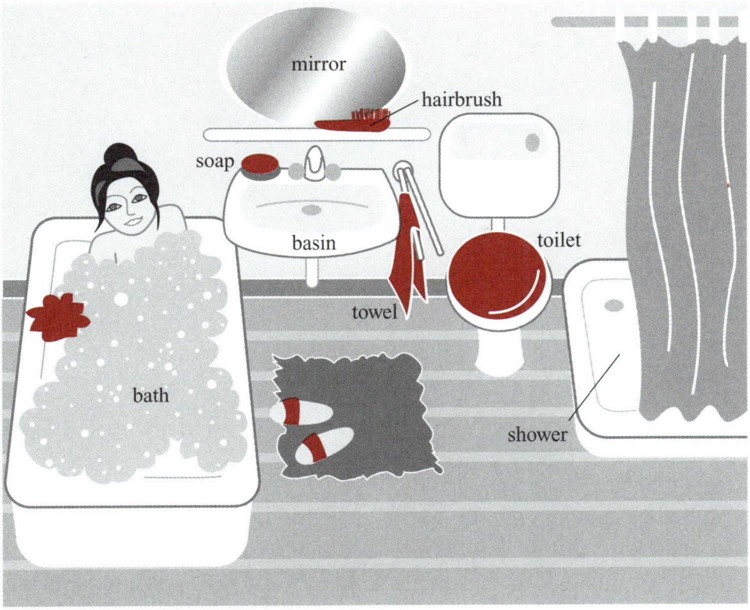

As she lay in the bath, her mind went over the events of the last two days. *Scoring* the goal during the hockey match had been a great triumph. Tracey had told her that the St. Mary's team went on to win the match after she had left the hockey field. Her goal had won the match and she was delighted with that. However, the *theft* of her precious *locket* had really upset her. First she had cried and now she was angry that someone had *dared* to steal her property. At first she had wrongly thought it was Giles, but after the second text message and the conversation with Tracey she was sure that it could not have been him. He would not have given himself away so easily. Now that Arthur's name had been mentioned she could see how he could have been behind the *theft*.

The more she thought about it, the more she was *convinced* that he was guilty. Her thoughts went back to the hockey match. Yes, that was it, she suddenly remembered. When she was injured he had made some comment about poor Susan being hurt. He had been standing nearby with that friend of his. Yes, thought Susan, he could easily have gone into the changing room during the match and taken the *locket* without anyone noticing.

! ÜBUNG 29

Übung 29: Lies weiter und unterstreiche die acht Adjektive im Text!

Some admirer, thought Susan. A *would-be* boyfriend who steals your property in order to play the hero!
When she had finished her hot bath Susan spent the rest of the morning tidying her bedroom. She went downstairs for lunch. Sunday lunch was always a big event. They always had a roast for lunch. Her father would not eat anything else, so Susan's mum always had to work in their kitchen to prepare the food. Dad spent most of the morning reading the Sunday paper. They were a very traditional family. Today it was roast beef and Yorkshire pudding. Susan's mum was a great cook and always made her own Yorkshire puddings, small round ones that tasted very good with *gravy*.

After lunch she went back up to her room and *texted* her friends.
As the weather was so nice they decided to meet in the park by the *swings* at three o'clock. Heather arrived first, closely followed by Tracey.
"Did anyone follow you?" Susan asked Tracey.
"No," answered Tracey.
"Are you sure?" continued Susan, anxious to know if the boys were still watching them.
"Well, I didn't notice anyone," said Tracey.
"And you, Heather?" asked Susan.

"Well, to be honest I didn't really look behind me, sorry," came the reply.
"Listen," said Susan, "in future we have to be more careful and always check that nobody is following us."
She turned to Heather and said: "I got another text message yesterday. Tracey knows as we met when you were out shopping with your mum," she continued in a sarcastic tone.

Übung 30: Schreibe die Zahlen aus!

ÜBUNG 30 !

1. 16 ______________________
2. 69 ______________________
3. 1/3 ______________________
4. 1,500 ______________________
5. 2,000,000 ______________________
6. 4th ______________________
7. 110 ______________________
8. 80 ______________________
9. 53 ______________________
10. 46 ______________________

"Okay," said Heather. "No need for you to be so *mean*. I do have a family as well, you know. I am not your personal servant!"
"Alright, alright," said Susan in a soft voice. "I'm sorry, it has all just been so stressful recently and I overreacted."
"Well, what was the message?" asked Heather finally.

Susan explained how the sender knew she had told someone about the *blackmail* as he or she had seen her with her friends. Heather agreed that they could now rule out Giles as he would not send a message so soon after she had spoken to him in the café. That would just be too obvious.

"So who do you think it is now? Who is the main suspect?" asked Heather.

"It was Tracey who gave me the idea," said Susan. "I am *convinced* now that it was Arthur. He and his friend George were at the hockey match and they were *spying on* us in the shopping centre. I'm sure it was him."

Heather also knew that Arthur was often hanging around Susan. She also agreed that he had a good reason to take the *locket* in order to make Giles look bad. His behaviour certainly looked *suspicious*. She remembered that she had seen Giles and Arthur fighting in the *playground* a while back; they were definitely not the best of friends.

"So what do we do now?" asked Heather.

"Well," said Susan. "We cannot approach Arthur until school tomorrow. If he really is behind this it will be no problem to get my *locket* off him. I mean he is not angry at me, he is trying to get a date with me after all!"

"True," said Heather. "We can certainly *tackle* him easily. I think we should get him alone in the *playground* and make him tell us everything. Girlpower – that's what we need!" They all laughed together.

It was good to laugh after what they had been through over the last few days. Things had been very tense. The idea that they might be able to solve the mystery together really *cheered* them *up*.

"We will certainly make him suffer for all this!" said Tracey. "I mean, *what a cheek* stealing your *locket* just to get a date!"

Übung 31: Lies weiter und unterstreiche im folgenden Textabschnitt die Synonyme der Wörter in Klammern!
(1. saw, 2. shouted, 3. certainly, 4. usually, 5. stood up, 6. discover)

Suddenly Susan looked up and noticed two figures coming into the park.
"Oh no, look who's coming!" she cried out.
Heather and Tracey looked across and saw two girls walking up the hill and towards the *bench* where they were sitting.
"It's Amanda and Beverly," said Susan.
"What are they doing here?" said Tracey.
"I think they've seen us," said Heather.
At that moment the two girls, Amanda and Beverly, stopped and looked across to where the three friends were sitting. They had definitely been *spotted*.
"Do you think they have been *spying on* us?" said Heather. "They normally never come in the park. What are they doing here today?"
Susan got up and said:
"Come on, I'm going to find out what they want."

Susan started walking *boldly* across the grass to where the other girls were standing.
"No, wait!" said Heather, pulling Susan's *sleeve*. "Look, they are leaving already!"
The two girls had obviously changed their minds and were now *heading* down the bank.
"Very strange," said Heather. "What are they up to now?"
"I don't know, but I'm not waiting around here to find out," said Susan. "Come on, let's catch them up."
This time Heather followed Susan obediently. She saw that Susan was determined to follow the girls. She turned to Tracey and said:

"Come on, you come, too. We have to stay together."

As fast as they could, the three girls made their way down the bank towards the bottom of the park.

"Hey!" shouted Susan. "What are you doing, *spying on* us?"

Now Beverly turned. She realized that she had been *spotted* and there was no longer the chance to get away unnoticed.

"What's it got to do with you?" she said in an angry voice.

She moved closer to her friend Amanda for support. Although she was taller than Susan she saw that Susan had her two friends with her and she did not like *being outnumbered*. However, she was confident that she could beat Susan one on one and so she decided to go for the attack:

"You don't own this park. Anyone can come here!" she said in a really sarcastic voice. She walked towards Susan until they were *facing* each other *eyeball to eyeball*.

Susan was now really frightened. She was *convinced* that Beverly and Amanda had been *spying on* her. Susan bit her lip, put her hands on her hips and took a deep breath.

"What is it you want, Beverly Little? Why are you coming here and *spying on* us?"

Suddenly Beverly's face went red and in a rage she ran towards Susan. She realized that Susan had discovered her *spying*. Her *fists* were *clenched* and she was on the attack.

"You little *bitch*!" she screamed.

In a flash she was on top of Susan and the two of them were scratching and pulling each other's hair. A real fight had started. Susan struggled to defend herself, but she *was* no *match for* Beverly.

"Stop!" cried Heather. She fell to the floor and tried to pull the two girls apart. Tracey stood back horrified and did not know what to do. She had seen girls fight before and it was not a pretty sight. She wanted to dive in to help Susan, but fear kept her from moving.

She couldn't feel her legs and couldn't move.
Meanwhile Amanda had joined in and was now *helping* Beverly *to her feet*. Beverly's face was *bleeding* where Susan had scratched her. Susan was *rubbing* her sore head, and she had been scratched on the face as well.

Übung 32: Welche Ergänzung ist die richtige? Kreuze an!

ÜBUNG 32 !

1. Susan is a good hockey player,
   a) ☐ doesn't she?
   b) ☐ isn't she?

2. Arthur likes Susan,
   a) ☐ doesn't he?
   b) ☐ do he?

3. The locket was stolen,
   a) ☐ ain't it?
   b) ☐ wasn't it?

4. They met in the park,
   a) ☐ didn't they?
   b) ☐ weren't they?

5. You know the answer,
   a) ☐ aren't you?
   b) ☐ don't you?

Beverly was shaking. She was furious.
"You haven't heard the last of this, Susan Wilson!" she screamed.

"Just wait! I will get my revenge! You will be so sorry that you ever touched me! I will make you pay for this!"

The two girls then turned and disappeared from the park.

Tracey now came over to Susan.

"Sorry, sorry Susan," she stammered. "I just froze. I couldn't move. I don't know what came over me."

"She is a really *mean bitch*!" said Heather. "She came at you like an angry bull. Are you sure you're okay?"

Susan sat up and *rubbed* her head again.

"I'm okay, nothing broken. Just a bit of shock, that's all," she said.

Her friends *helped* her *to her feet* and they went over and sat on the *bench* again. Heather and Tracey wanted to take her to the hospital, but Susan said they were overreacting. She just wanted to sit for a while and get her breath back.

"Don't tell my parents about this, will you?" she said to her two friends. "I have to keep all this quiet until I know for sure who has got the *locket*."

ÜBUNG 33 !

Übung 33: Beantworte die Fragen zum Text!

1. What did Tracey do while Susan was fighting with Beverly?

2. Where on her body was Susan hurt?

3. Where did Heather and Tracey want to go with Susan?

4. Who is Beverly's friend?

5. Does Susan want to tell her parents about the fight?

"Well, those two certainly *have it in for* you," said Heather. "Beverly especially seems to *hate your guts*!"
"Yes," said Susan. "She obviously came here looking for trouble. I have never liked that girl and I'm certainly glad to *see the back of* her."
"In future maybe we shouldn't *hang around* in the park," said Heather. "They could come back with more friends next time. We don't want any more trouble."
"Agreed," replied Susan. "We need to find a safer place to meet. Can we go over to your place, Tracey?" she asked.
Tracey agreed and the three friends then walked over to Tracey's house. Luckily her parents had gone out so they had the place to themselves.
"That's cool," said Susan. "Let's agree a plan of action for tomorrow. Where does Arthur *hang out* in the first break?"
"He's always by the ping-pong tables," said Tracey.
"Okay then," said Susan. "Let's meet in the first break and get him on his own. The three of us will soon find out what he is hiding."
"But if he does have the *locket* he is not going to admit it," said Heather.
"Don't worry. I will make sure he *confesses*," said Susan. "If we all stick together," she added, glancing across at Tracey, "he *isn't a match for* us, believe me!"
The three girls spent the rest of the afternoon chatting and playing CDs. They discussed various ways to get the truth out of Arthur. They were sure that the three of them would be able to *pressure* him

into telling the truth. If he had taken the *locket*, then they would force it out of him. They thought that surprise was the best option.

Chapter 5: Unexpected Help

Normally Susan hated Monday mornings and going back to school, but today was different. She just could not wait to get to school. At last she had the chance to confront Arthur. She had to find out if he was behind all this. Quickly she ate her cornflakes and drank her orange juice before catching the bus to school. Tracey was on the same bus and Susan was really pleased to see her. When they arrived at St. Mary's they went to the *playground* and met up with Heather.

"Has anyone seen Arthur yet?" asked Susan.

"Yes, I saw him arrive with his *mate* George earlier," said Heather.

"Good, well done," said Susan. "Right, don't forget. We meet at first break by the canteen exit."

The first two lessons were double biology. Susan spent a lot of her time staring out of the window. She could just not concentrate. At one point the teacher, Mrs Henderson, asked her a question about the reproduction organs of eagles. Susan had awoken with a jump and the whole class had laughed at her. Normally that would have *bothered* her, but today she had only one thought in mind: to get hold of Arthur.

ÜBUNG 34 !

Übung 34: Welche Gegenteile gehören zusammen? Ordne zu!

1. ☐ excited	a) different
2. ☐ quickly	b) difficult

3. ☐ same c) find
4. ☐ far d) slowly
5. ☐ hide e) wrong
6. ☐ easy f) bored
7. ☐ right g) near

When the bell rang for first break, Susan packed up her things and left the class as soon as possible. Tracey and Heather were in a different class for biology so she met them in the *playground*.

"So, are we all ready?" asked Susan in an excited voice.

"Sure thing," said Tracey.

"Me too," said Heather.

"Let's go and find him then," replied Susan.

The three girls *set off* for the table tennis area. They moved slowly as they wanted to see Arthur before he saw them. It was important to get him alone.

"Look!" cried Heather. "There he is, over by the second table."

Sure enough Arthur has *hanging around* chatting to some friends by the tables.

"Right," said Susan. "This is what I suggest: Tracey, you go over and tell him that you need to talk to him in private. Get him to follow you over to the trees in the far corner of the *playground*. Heather and I can hide behind the *dustbins* and when you get there we can surprise him. Is that agreed?"

"Yeah, good idea," said Tracey. "It will be best to get him on his own. I will make up some story to get his interest. It will be easy, just watch me!"

Heather agreed and she went with Susan to hide behind the school *dustbins*. They were a bit smelly, but it was a great place to hide as no-one ever went there and there was a *courtyard* where they could *trap* Arthur. They could then question him without being disturbed.

As soon as they were out of sight, Tracey slowly walked over towards the ping-pong tables. She waited for a while until Arthur had finished talking to his friends and then quickly made a move from behind. She tapped him on the shoulder and said:
"Excuse me, Arthur, I need to talk to you."
"Eh, what?" exclaimed Arthur, very surprised that someone should be talking to him. A girl even! And a pretty one, too. He was both delighted and shocked at the same time. In fact he was speechless. Tracey took the initiative and continued speaking.
"In private. I really need to talk to you in private."
"About what?" said Arthur, now he had found his voice again.
"I can't mention it here. It is something very personal," said Tracey. She looked him straight in the eyes and tried to look as loving as possible. Arthur was totally shocked and when she put her arm in his, he happily gave in and followed her across the *playground*.
Was this really happening to him? He could hardly believe it. He felt he should speak and say something clever or impressive, but nothing came to mind. At one point when he tried to speak, Tracey turned to him with a finger on her lips and said:
"Shush, not here, wait!"
So he did not say a word and allowed Tracey to lead him across the *playground*. He had no idea what she wanted from him and he was anxious to find out. Tracey turned the corner by the tree and as she did so Susan and Heather jumped out from their hiding place.
"Hi, Arthur," said Susan in very *stern* voice. "We have something we want to speak with you about!"
Suddenly Arthur realized that he was surrounded by three girls. Was he dreaming or was this an *ambush*? Before he had a chance to speak, Susan stepped out and said:
"We need to talk, Arthur!"
She led him into the corner behind the *dustbins* and Arthur realized

he was *trapped*. His first thought was to push past the three girls and to run away, but then he thought: I haven't done anything wrong. Why should I have to run away? It would be better to stay and *face* them.

"What's going on?" he cried. "Is this some kind of *ambush* or what?"

Susan looked him straight in the eyes. She was not going to *back down* now and she was determined to make him tell the truth.

"Something of mine has gone missing!" she said and waited for his reaction. Arthur looked puzzled.

"Something of mine that is very precious has been taken and I want to know if you took it," she said. "Do you know what I am talking about, Arthur? Someone has been sending me messages and I need to know who it is."

ÜBUNG 35 !

Übung 35: Lies weiter und unterstreiche die acht Wörter, die falsch geschrieben sind. Verbessere sie anschließend!

Arthur stared at Susan with a blank expression on his face. He had no idea what she was tolking about and actually he was getting quite frightened now. Susan to was surprised at his reaction and started to wonder if he wos perhaps innocent after all. He made no effort to defend himself and really seemed to have no idea what she was talking about. Susan decided to continue to make sure.
"Someone has stealed my *locket* and is *blackmailing* me," she sad.
"And you think I had something to do with this?" said Arthur with a look of *amazement* on his face. "I sware I had no idea your *locket* had been stolen, or that you were being *blackmailed*. Really, you have to beleive me, Susan. I would never do anything to hurt you."
Susan saw that tears were beginning to *rise up* in Arthur's eyes. He really did seem to be telling the truth.
"But what were you doing in the shopping centre? Why where you following us?" said Susan.

1. ______________________ 5. ______________________

2. ______________________ 6. ______________________

3. ______________________ 7. ______________________

4. ______________________ 8. ______________________

"We were just there by chance," said Arthur. "George and I often go there. When we saw you coming out of the billiard café looking so sad I just wondered what was up. That's all. I'm telling the truth, Susan, honestly."
"I have an idea," interrupted Tracey. "We should check his *mobile*

number. That way we can know if he sent the messages."
"Great idea, Tracey, good thinking," said Susan.
"Come on then, Arthur, show us your *mobile*," she continued.
"Sure," said Arthur. "Anything to show that I am innocent."
Obediently Arthur took out his *mobile*. Susan then took out hers and opened the messages section.
"Now if I reply to the *blackmail* message we will know for sure if you sent it!" said Susan triumphantly.
"But then if it's not Arthur, the *blackmailer* will get the message instead," said Tracey.
"Good point," said Susan. "Okay, we have to make it a serious message then. What shall I write?" she asked.
"Hmm, let me think a bit," said Heather. "How about – I know who you are!"
"No way," said Susan. "That might *scare* him *off* and I would never see the *locket* again."
"Well, write something about the money then," said Tracey. "How about – I need more time to get the money."
"Just a moment," said Susan. "He said not to contact him, so that might cause more trouble. Not a very good idea."
Then suddenly Susan had another idea.
"I don't need to write a proper message, you know. I could just type in a few letters and press send. You know, pretend it was sent by mistake. That way the *blackmailer* would not know what was going on and would just think it was a technical fault."
"Great idea!" said Heather. "That way he cannot suspect anything."
So Susan took the phone and typed 'ntee'. Then she pressed the 'Send' button. At the same time she held Arthur's *mobile* in her other hand. She waited and waited, but no sound came from the phone at all.
"Well," said Susan and she turned to look at Arthur. "It does seem

that you are telling the truth after all."

"Look, Susan, maybe I can help," said Arthur. He was now beginning to feel confident again. Actually, he would do anything for Susan and saw his chance to win her friendship.

"Has someone really stolen your *locket*? Are you really being *blackmailed*?" he said in a very concerned voice.

Susan thought for a moment. Arthur now knew what was going on anyway. There was *no point in denying* it and maybe he might even be able to help them.

"Look, Arthur," said Susan, now much calmer. "I'm really sorry we accused you. I see now that you had nothing to do with all this."

"It's okay," said Arthur. "No bad feelings. I just want to help, that's all."

Susan looked at Tracey, then Heather. They both nodded their heads in agreement.

"Well," began Susan. "It was like this…"

She then continued to tell the story of how the *locket* was stolen and about the ultimatum that came by text message. Next she told him about the *showdown* with Giles and then the fight with Beverly.

"But that's awful!" exclaimed Arthur when she had finished. "No wonder you were *upset*. Look, I really think I can help you with this. Don't you think it would be good to have a *guy* on your side?"

Susan and Heather laughed. Was Arthur trying to play the Romeo now?

! ÜBUNG 36

Übung 36: Bilde das Simple Past dieser Verben!

1. to go ____________

2. to find ____________

3. to see ____________

4. to tell ____________

5. to lose ____________

6. to do ____________

7. to say ____________

8. to know ____________

"Well," said Susan after a while. "It would be good to have some help. We still have to find a way to *raise* two hundred *quid* by Friday!"

Susan told her friends that she had seventy-five pounds in her post office savings account. That was all the savings she had. She did not want to lose the money, but saw no other way.

Arthur felt pleased now he saw that he would be able to join in the little gang. He would do anything for Susan and he intended to get back her *locket at all costs*.

"We have to work together to get the *blackmail* money. That is certain," he said. "Otherwise your *locket* will be gone, Susan. The *blackmailer* is certain to destroy the *locket* or get rid of it somehow if he doesn't get the money."

"No! No!" said Susan, now sounding very scared. "I must get that *locket* back; it means the world to me!"

"Now, now," said Arthur. "Calm down. There may be another way. Maybe when we hand over the cash we can somehow catch the *blackmailers*. They will be expecting you to come alone. However, if we have enough people to help us, then perhaps we can jump on them when they pick up the cash."

Susan started to feel a *glimmer of hope*.

"But who would you get to help?" she asked.

"And we are not supposed to tell anyone, remember!" remarked Tracey.

"Well, you've already told me now, haven't you," said Arthur. "And the *blackmailer* knows about Tracey and Heather, too. I would just suggest we include my *mate* George. He is a big strong *lad* and would come in very useful."

"Well," said Susan. "I can *see* your *point*. A bit of muscle power would be a good idea. What do you think, girls?" she said, turning to the other two.

! ÜBUNG 37

Übung 37: In diesen Sätzen sind die Wörter durcheinander geraten. Bringe sie in die richtige Reihenfolge und beachte dabei auch Satzzeichen und Groß- und Kleinschreibung!

1. friend is Heather good of Susan's a

2. locket someone stolen the has

3. scored a goal Susan

4. felt rise Susan hope

5. toffees floor the on fell the

6. is Tracey who

7. to there explanation has be an

8. message she text a sent

"What have we got to lose?" asked Heather.
Tracey was not so sure at first. She was worried about too many people being involved. Also she seemed mistrustful of Arthur, but eventually the other two girls persuaded her and she agreed to ask George for help.
"But he doesn't need to know all the details," she said. "Arthur, can't you tell him you need him for a mission on Friday, without telling him any more details? Just make up some story. We can't risk involving too many people," said Tracey.
"Yes, you *have a point*, Tracey," said Susan. "It would be good to keep this to ourselves until the last minute."
"Sure," said Arthur. "I can manage that. I will tell him we have some business to take care of on Friday and I will give him the full details later. You can *rely on* me. I will keep your secret."
Susan looked at Arthur as he spoke. She realized that she had been wrong about him. A short while ago she had *ambushed* him and was questioning him. Now here he was offering to help and to get his friend to assist, too. Maybe he was not such a loser after all. It was amazing that help often came from the most unlikely places.
"Thanks, Arthur," said Susan. "You really are a big help. I'm really sorry for how I treated you. I was wrong to suspect you and I apologize. I feel really bad."

Arthur started to *blush*. Susan's kind words and soft tone of voice had made him quite *embarrassed*.

"No problem," he replied quickly. He tried hard to hide his embarrassment. Then he changed the subject to *divert attention*.

"Now what about the money? How are we going to *raise* two hundred *quid* in cash by Friday? Susan has seventy-five pounds, what about the rest of you?" said Arthur.

"Well, I don't have much savings," said Heather. "Not more than fifty pounds, I would say."

"Thanks, Heather," said Susan. "That's *real nice* of you, but I couldn't possibly take all your savings from you."

"Look, Susan, you're not taking anything. It's just a *loan*, that's all. I'm getting the money back, aren't I? I mean, we are all getting our money back. That's the idea, isn't it?" She looked across at Arthur for confirmation.

"Yes, certainly!" replied Arthur. "If our plan works, sorry, I mean, when our plan works, we will all get our money back."

"Your money, too?" snapped Tracey. "Are you also willing to put up some cash?"

"Well, I haven't got much, but I could manage say about twenty *quid*," Arthur replied.

"Is that all?" said Tracey sarcastically. "Do you think you can buy Susan's friendship with only twenty pounds?" she continued.

"Now hold on, Tracey!" interrupted Susan. "No need to be so *mean* to Arthur. I am grateful for all the help I can get. What were you thinking of contributing anyway?"

Susan looked at Tracey. She knew that Tracey had *loads of* money. At school she always wore the latest fashions and her parents lived in that big *mansion*-style house.

"Well," said Tracey, calming down a little. "I'm sure I can manage fifty pounds as well."

Übung 38: Welche der Erklärungen stimmt? Kreuze die richtige Lösung an!

1. I couldn't possibly take them.
   a) ☐ I don't want to take them.
   b) ☐ Maybe I'll take them.

2. Are you also willing to put up some cash?
   a) ☐ Will you steal some money?
   b) ☐ Will you give us some money?

3. I could manage twenty quid.
   a) ☐ I could provide twenty pounds.
   b) ☐ I could earn twenty pounds.

4. How much were you thinking to contribute?
   a) ☐ Have you any good ideas?
   b) ☐ What will you give?

"Great!" said Susan. "That makes one hundred and ninety-five pounds in total. I can easily borrow another five pounds from my dad and then we will have all the money we need."
Tracey was now having doubts about handing over the cash. Although Susan was her best friend, Tracey was always a bit *tight* with spending money. She did not want to appear *mean* in front of Arthur, but she really did not want to part with the money. Then she had an idea.
"How about using false notes?" she said. "My dad has a really super copier. We could copy some twenty pound notes and mix them in with the real ones," she said.
"No," said Arthur. "That would not work. They are sure to notice. I

mean, we are not professional *forgers*. The banknotes we make would not be good enough to *fool* them."

"Nice idea though!" added Susan, trying to save the situation. "Well, can you all check that you do have those amounts and let's meet back here again tomorrow. Shall we say at 10.30 a.m. here again?"

"Yes, that's cool with me," said Tracey.

"Me too," said Heather.

"Yes, I can make it as well," said Arthur. "No problem."

"Look, Arthur," said Susan. "Maybe you had better go back into the *playground* alone. I think it's best if we are not seen together to *avoid suspicion*."

Arthur was disappointed. He had rather hoped he could *hang around* with Susan and spend more time with her. But he realized that what she said made sense.

"Okay," he replied. "I will *head* on back to my *mates* and will meet you here tomorrow. See you then," he said. Then he turned and made his way back to the *playground*.

"Are you sure we can trust him?" said Tracey, as soon as he was out of sight.

"He seems *genuine* to me," said Susan.

"Me too," said Heather. "I mean, he didn't have to offer to help us. After the way we treated him he had every right to be angry with us."

"I have a good feeling about Arthur," replied Susan. "I am *convinced* he is going to be a great help to us and we definitely need help if we are going to *recover* my *locket* safely."

"Well, I still think we should keep a close eye on him," said Tracey, sounding very doubtful.

"Don't worry," said Susan. "We will watch him closely and make sure he does exactly what we ask him to. Now come on, it's time to get back inside or we will be late."

The three friends left their hiding place behind the *dustbins* and walked back across the *playground*. In the distance Susan saw the familiar figures of Beverly and Amanda. She slowed her *pace*; she did not want to *face* them again today. However, it was only a question of time before she would have to confront them. The school was only a small place and she could not *avoid* them forever. The rest of the day passed without event. Susan felt as if she was in a dream.

Übung 39: Finde die neuen Wörter!

1. Change a letter in LOOK to prepare a meal. COOK
2. Change a letter in BARK to find a place to meet. ______
3. Change a letter in ROCKET to make an item of jewellery. ______
4. Change a letter in RIGHT to make it dark. ______
5. Change a letter in ROUND to make English money. ______
6. Change a letter in BAD to make an item of furniture. ______

Susan could not concentrate during the lessons and in maths Mrs Fisher *told* her *off* twice for not paying attention. At lunchtime she sat with Heather and Tracey as usual, but she did not finish her lunch and did not feel hungry. If Arthur was innocent who else could have taken her *locket*, she thought. Giles too had been excluded *due to* the timing of the text message after their *show-*

down. So that only left Beverly and Amanda. The fight in the park had shaken her and at the time she had forgotten about the *locket*. But now she thought about it, she realized that the two of them could easily have taken her *locket* and sent the text messages. But how could she prove it? She certainly could not approach them directly – she needed someone else to help. Her thoughts were interrupted suddenly:

"Hey Susan!" said Heather. "Are you falling asleep over your pie and chips?"

"Eh, what, oh sorry!" said Susan.

"You seem to be far away," said Heather.

"I was just thinking about who else could have taken the *locket*."

"And who do you think?"

Übung 40: Sind die folgenden Aussagen richtig? Markiere mit richtig ✔ oder falsch – !

ÜBUNG 40 !

1. If something is not difficult, you can do it easily. ☐
2. If you seem to be far away, you aren't concentrating. ☐
3. A teacher likes pupils who don't pay attention. ☐
4. Innocent is the opposite of guilty. ☐
5. Agreeing on something means being of a different opinion. ☐
6. If you are shaken by something, you are brave. ☐

"I can only think of Beverly and Amanda, they certainly acted very strangely in the park."

The other two agreed.

"We have to work out a plan how to find out if they stole the *locket*," said Heather. "And we need someone who knows them to help us."

"I know. How about asking Arthur? They won't suspect him."

Heather agreed that it was a good idea. Tracey was not sure at first, but eventually agreed that it was the best idea.

"In the meantime we have to work on getting the money together," said Susan. "Don't forget: we're meeting tomorrow to *sort out* the money."

They all nodded and went back to their afternoon classes.

Chapter 6: Beg, Borrow or Steal

Later that day after her evening meal at around 6 p.m., Tracey went up to her room. She had a secret hiding place where she kept all her banknotes. It was in a pink *pouch* at the bottom of her *wardrobe*. After a few minutes she found the *pouch* and took it out. She sat on

the bed and counted her savings. She had thirty-five pounds and twenty pence.
Oh dear, she thought. I told Susan I would give her fifty pounds. What am I going to do now? She knew that Susan would be disappointed if she could not lend her the amount she promised. There had to be a way to borrow the money. And who could she ask? Her dad was always the best option. She just had to think of an excuse why she needed the money.
She had often borrowed money in the past from her dad, sometimes for clothes, for trips to the cinema and for other essential items like shoes, handbags and make-up. Being a teenager was an expensive business and her monthly *pocket money* of fifty pounds just never seemed to last until the end of the month.

! ÜBUNG 41

Übung 41: Trage die fehlenden Buchstaben ein!

1. You play h _ _ k _ _ with a stick.
2. A lot of people is a cr _ _ d.
3. Your arm is attached to your sh _ _ _ d _ r.
4. Susan was bl _ _ km _ _ _ _ d.
5. The locket was a pr _ _ _ _ t from her grandmother.
6. Pupils in England wear a school u _ _ f _ _ _.
7. Was the sender an _ ny _ _ _ s?
8. She was tired and y _ _ n _ _.

She looked at herself in the mirror. In her old sweatshirt and jogging trousers she did not look her best. To get her dad's attention she had better smarten up a bit. She looked through her *wardrobe* and took out her favourite pink blouse; her dad always liked her in that. Next she put on her black jeans. She had already learned various tricks for persuading her dad when she wanted something. She looked in the mirror one last time and walked slowly down the stairs.

Her father was sitting on the sofa watching football on TV. Luckily her mum was in the kitchen washing the dishes and so she could speak to him alone.

"Hi dad!" she said in her sweetest voice and sat down beside him. He continued to watch the TV and just *mumbled*.

"Hi."

Tracey was not going to give up easily.

"Good game?" she asked, trying to show an interest in what he was watching.

"Er, what?" he replied.

"I said is it a good game?" asked Tracey patiently.

"Yeah, Chelsea are winning one nil," he answered.

Tracey was pleased. Her dad was a big Chelsea fan and if his team was winning then he was sure to be in a good mood.

"Dad," she said slowly, building up to the big question.

"What is it you want this time?" her father answered. He knew his only daughter well and knew when she wanted something.

Übung 42: Vervollständige die Sätze mit ***his, him, she*** *oder* ***her****!*

ÜBUNG 42 !

1. Susan was worried when ________ locket was stolen.

2. George was pleased to help ________ friend Arthur.

3. Susan's mum thought ________ should go to the doctor.

4. Giles was annoyed when Susan finished with ________.

5. Tracey tried to get money off ________ dad.

"The thing is I need a new pair of boots for hockey," said Tracey. Her boots were fine, but this was the best excuse she could think of to get some money from her dad. However, her father was not so easily *fooled*.

"Hockey boots?" he said. "What's wrong with your old boots? Didn't we buy you a new pair just a few months ago?"

Tracey had to think quickly: "Well, they are already really worn out and scratched. They are uncomfortable, too. I really need a new pair," she said. She was trying hard to think of a way to persuade her father to hand over the money.

"That's funny," said her father. "Have you only just realized they are uncomfortable after you have been wearing them for several months? Maybe I should have a look at them."

"Alright," said Tracey. She now realized that her father was not as easily *fooled* as she thought. Maybe she should tell the truth after all. But no, that would not work. What about her promise to Susan not to tell anyone? Could she trust her parents not to report this to the police? No, she thought. She could not *take* that *risk*; she would have to think of some other excuse for needing the money.

"You win!" she said *reluctantly*. "I don't really need new hockey boots. I just need some money."

"And why?" asked her father *expectantly*.

"Well, it's for Susan, you see." Tracey started talking and then she had a brilliant idea. She could mention the *locket*, but pretend that it was only broken and had to be repaired!

"Go on," said her father. He now seemed more interested. Usually his daughter asked for money to buy clothes, make-up or shoes.

This was the first time she was asking for money for somebody else.
"Susan has a big problem," said Tracey. "She has broken a really *valuable locket*. It was a present from her grandmother, a family *heirloom*. The chain snapped and it will cost a lot of money to repair it."
Tracey was really pleased with herself. This is a good story she thought, it is not all a lie and the money really is for Susan.
"Can't her parents pay for the repairs?" said her dad.
"No, that's just the problem. You see, she broke the chain in a fight with another girl. If her parents find out they will be really *cross* with her. They are very strict, you know." Again Tracey felt almost triumphant. This was a really good story she was making up.
Her father stopped watching the match and looked at her to see if she was telling the truth. His daughter had been friends with Susan for many years, ever since junior school in fact. So it did seem normal that she would want to help Susan. He also knew that Susan's parents were not *well-off* and so they might be very angry if she had damaged a *valuable* piece of jewellery.
"Wow, I'm really touched," said her dad. "That is really kind of you to help Susan to *raise* the money for the repair. Is anybody else helping?"
Tracey explained how Heather was also helping. She said that Heather had offered to lend Susan fifty pounds.
"Fifty pounds!" her father exclaimed. "How much does the repair cost?"
Tracey *hesitated* for a moment. If she said two hundred pounds her father would never believe her.
"About ninety pounds," she said quickly. She realized that she had made a big mistake by saying fifty. "You see, Susan is really *broke* and the most she can get is twenty pounds."

ÜBUNG 43 !

Übung 43: Setze das entsprechende Verb im Present Perfect ein!

1. *Has* she *found* the money? (find)
2. __________ you ________________ another jeweller? (try)
3. __________ they ________________ to the billiard café? (be)
4. __________ I ________________ the locket before? (see)
5. __________ it ________________ from your bag? (disappear)
6. __________ we ________________ the boy? (meet)
7. __________ she ________________ her parents? (tell)
8. __________ he ________________ a message? (receive)
9. __________ you ________________ a new pair of hockey boots? (buy)

"Have you asked around different jewellers to get the *locket* repaired?" her father said. "Maybe you can get it done cheaper somewhere else?"

"Yeah, great idea, dad," said Tracey quickly. "Why didn't we think of that? Tell you what: I will discuss it with the others tomorrow. But for now can you lend me twenty pounds?"

"Well, alright, I suppose so," her dad said. "But I am only lending it to you, remember. I will take it out of your *pocket money* for next month."

"Okay," said Tracey *reluctantly*. She had hoped he might just give her the money, but at least he was lending it to her. After all, she intended to get the money back from Susan anyway. It was only a *loan*, she told herself.

"Thanks, dad," she said and threw her arms around him. She *gave* him *a* big *hug* and a kiss. "You're the best!" she added. It was a bit *over the top* she thought, but at least she had got what she wanted.

Her dad took out his wallet and handed over a twenty-pound note. "Now," he said. "Maybe I can go back to watching the match again?"

"Yeah, sure, dad," said Tracey. "I'll just go back up to my room and watch *telly* for a bit."

With a feeling of delight Tracey turned around and raced up the stairs. She shut her bedroom door and crashed down on the bed.

She was so excited that she decided to *text* Susan straightaway.

Her phone was on her bedside table. She picked it up and pressed the key pad to type in her message: "have *yr* money – all of it! *c u 2moro, lol* tracey". Then she pressed the 'Send' button.

Meanwhile Susan was also in her bedroom trying to concentrate on the maths homework. When she heard the message tone she reached over and grabbed her phone. At first she thought it might be another message from the *blackmailers*. She was very relieved when she saw the name 'Tracey' in the display.

After reading her message she felt much happier. At last the money was being *gathered* together. Tomorrow she would take her post office *savings book* to school. Then she could go straight after school to the local post office and *withdraw* the money. Seventy-five pounds was a lot of money. Maybe she should take her friends with her to support her, especially if someone else might be watching her. She was still very worried that she might meet Beverly and Amanda alone somewhere.

She typed a message to Tracey: "*gr8, thx. c u* at school. *lol* susan". Then she pressed the 'Send' button.

She went back to her maths homework and now the sums seemed much easier. It would soon be bedtime and she wanted to get the calculations finished before she went to bed. At least Mrs Fisher would be happy if she got all these done, she thought. She did not want to cause any more trouble.

ÜBUNG 44 !

Übung 44: Setze das richtige Fragewort ein!

1. ________________ old are you?
2. ________________ took the locket?
3. ________________ one do you prefer?
4. ________________ much homework do we have?
5. ________________ did you lose it? During the game?
6. ________________ did you hide? In the bushes?
7. ________________ is the best thing to do?
8. ________________ hates me so much?

Heather, however, did not find it so easy to get her share of the money. When she got home she went straight to her room to check her *savings book*. She usually kept it in the *drawer* of her writing desk. It was not there. Where could it be? She searched through all four of the *drawers*, but could not find it anywhere. In her frustration she emptied the contents of all the *drawers* onto her bed. There were books, magazines, *stationery* and photo albums spread all over her bed. She even put them all into piles to try to *sort* them *out*, but she could not find her *savings book* anywhere.
Oh no, she thought. What have I done with it? And what do I tell Susan? She is depending on me. I suppose I will have to go to the bank and tell them I have lost my *savings book*, but it may take a while to get a new one. I really need to help Susan, but what can I do?
In desperation she sat down on the bed and cried. She felt so desperate. She did not want to let Susan down, but how could she get fifty pounds in such a short time?

Then an idea came to her.
Her dad had a secret hiding place for banknotes in his desk, she thought. Maybe she could borrow the money and put it back before he noticed it? It was not really stealing the money, was it? She was going to put it back and he would never know. It was a risky plan and if she got caught there would be trouble, but she could not think of a better way.
Her parents normally came up to say goodnight to her at around 9 p.m. When her mum came up she pretended to be asleep. The bedroom door was open. Her mum knocked gently and there was no answer. She put her head to the door and whispered "Goodnight, Heather", but Heather did not reply. Luckily her mother then closed the door quietly behind her.
Later Heather heard her parents going to bed. She looked at her alarm clock. It was 10.30 p.m. She had found it hard to stay awake and she had put a *torch* under her *duvet* to read with. First she had to be sure that they were asleep. Her father *snored* and usually this annoyed her, but tonight she was glad of it. It was one way to make sure he was sound asleep. She read some more of her book and then checked the clock. It was now 11 p.m.
"Here goes," she whispered to herself. It should be all quiet now, she thought.

Übung 45: Beantworte die Fragen zum Text!

1. What did the thief want from Susan?

____

2. When was the locket stolen?

____

3. Which boys helped Susan and her friends?

4. Who is Giles?

5. Who lends Tracey twenty pounds?

Heather opened her bedroom door and *tiptoed* along the *hallway* to her parents' room. The door was open and she could hear her dad *snoring*. But what about her mum? She put her head through the *gap* and whispered: "Mum? Mum? Are you awake?"
She waited, but no answer came.
After pausing for a few minutes she decided it was safe to go downstairs. She walked very slowly and carefully as the stairs sometimes *creaked*. She had to make as little noise as possible.
When she reached the bottom of the stairs she turned left and walked into her father's study. His writing desk was up against the wall to the left of the window. Heather moved slowly across the room and shone her *torch* on the desk. Fortunately it was unlocked. She had often seen her dad put banknotes in a tin in the top right-hand *drawer* of the desk. Her dad did not know that Heather had often watched him and she knew his hiding place. Her fingers now trembled as she searched for the container. It was an old cigar box. Carefully she placed it on the desk and opened it. Quickly she counted the banknotes inside – one hundred and twenty-five pounds.
Heather told herself that she was going to put it back, and her dad wouldn't notice. She counted up fifty pounds, two twenty-pound notes and one ten-pound note. It's for Susan, she told herself. My friend needs my help and I will not let her down.

Once she had the cash safely in the pocket of her pyjamas, she *crept* back up the stairs. Her parents' room was still quiet, except for the sound of *snoring*. Poor mum, she thought, she must need *earplugs* to sleep with all that noise. She closed her bedroom door and then hid the money in her purse in the top *drawer* of her *chest of drawers*. Then she pulled back the covers from her bed and jumped in. In no time she was asleep, but she slept badly and had a nightmare. In her dream her father came into the room with a dark stranger and demanded her to return the money. It was a terrible nightmare. She felt so guilty for stealing the money, but she did not know how else she could help Susan.

Next morning Heather awoke with a shock. She had been *sweating* in the night and her pyjamas were wet with sweat. She looked under her bed, but there were no rats and she was definitely not in prison. It was just a nightmare, she thought, but she still felt really bad about taking the money. However, it was too late to put it back now and she had to help Susan to get her *locket* back, whatever the cost. Should she go to her father and *confess*? No, that would just cause more trouble. She would have to be brave and carry out her plan to the end. Her loyalty to Susan was important and there was no alternative.

ÜBUNG 46 !

Übung 46: Trage die fehlenden Buchstaben des beschriebenen Substantivs in die Lücken ein!

1. a different solution	_ lt _ _ n _ _ iv _
2. a bad dream	ni _ h _ m _ r _
3. to walk very quietly	t _ pt _ e
4. it covers you up at night	_ uv _ t
5. a kind of newspaper	_ a _ _ z _ n _
6. you keep your money in it	p _ _ s _
7. a light you hold in your hand	_ o _ c _
8. to make a loud noise when asleep	_ n _ r _

Because she slept badly Heather felt very tired. She decided to have a shower to freshen up. The warm water on her skin made her feel better and she dressed quickly for school. Her mum asked what she wanted for breakfast, but Heather was not hungry and said that she had a bad stomach ache.

"Maybe you should stay home today?" her mum asked. "Shall I write you a *sick note*?"

"Er, no, thanks. I'll be fine," said Heather. She simply had to get to school to tell Susan the news about the money.
As soon as she closed the front door she hurried along the road to catch the bus to school. As usual, Susan and Tracey were already on the bus and they all sat together. They talked about the weather, homework and what was on TV the night before, but they did not mention the money. They could not risk someone overhearing their conversation. At break time they all met behind the *dustbins* as agreed. Arthur was the last to arrive. Susan asked him to check that no-one was *spying on* them and reminded everybody to keep watch at all times.
"So, how did it go?" she asked. "Did you all get the money?"
"No problem!" said Tracey. "I had to borrow some from my dad. It wasn't easy at first, but I managed in the end."
"Thanks, Tracey, you are a real *mate*. I will pay you back when this is over. I promise!" said Susan.
Heather meanwhile was not looking so happy. She had been trying to smile and put on a brave face, but she felt so *exhausted*. She was not good at lying.
"*What's up*, Heather?" said Susan in a *compassionate* voice. She knew her friend well and felt something was wrong.
At that moment Heather *burst into tears*. Big hot tears rolled down her cheeks and she *sobbed* and *sobbed*. Susan put her arms around her and *hugged* her tight. Heather's body shook as she cried and it took a long while before she could speak.

Übung 47: Formuliere die folgenden Sätze im Passiv!

ÜBUNG 47 !

1. The blackmailer sent a text message.
A text message was sent by the blackmailer.

2. Heather stole the money.

____

3. Susan scored the goal.

____

4. Someone hated her.

____

5. Her parents looked after them.

____

6. The girls suspected Giles.

____

"I just can't do it!" she said and cried some more.
"What can't you do?" asked Susan.
"I can't keep on lying," she continued in a broken voice.
"About what?" said Susan.
"About the money," replied Heather. "I lost my *savings book* and I did not have any money so I took some from my dad's desk," she said. After she had told the truth she felt much better.
Now Tracey and Arthur also came over and both *comforted* Heather. She had a really bad conscience about taking the money.
"I think maybe I should put the money back."
The others agreed, and then Arthur came up with an offer of help.
"Don't worry," said Arthur. "We will *sort* this *out* somehow. You know I am sure that I can borrow some money from my parents like Tracey did. I can easily make up some story that I need to buy something. My dad is always generous."
He was not really sure if he could so easily borrow the money, but

he wanted to *reassure* Heather and to calm her down.
"Could you really?" said Heather. She was now much calmer. After she blew her nose she looked up at Arthur and said:
"Thanks! That would be really great!"
She *flung* her arms around Arthur and *gave* him *a* spontaneous *hug*. Arthur *blushed* and was very *embarrassed*.
"Sure!" he said. "No problem, I will get the money tomorrow!" Secretly he was not sure if he could get the fifty pounds, but he wanted to sound confident to impress Heather and above all to impress Susan.
"Wow, Arthur!" said Susan. "That is really *awesome!* If you can get the money that would solve the problem!"

Übung 48: Welches Wort ist das „schwarze Schaf"?

ÜBUNG 48 !

1. notice, see, observe, clock
2. school, playground, car, classroom
3. desk, quid, pounds, money
4. chest, drawers, shoulder, head
5. hockey, football, billiards, pitch
6. chocolate, sweets, teacher, ice cream
7. house, swing, mansion, flat

They agreed that Heather should return the money to her father's desk after school. He got home from work around 7 p.m., so she had lots of time to go into his study. It was important to do it when her mum was not looking, but that should be no problem. Susan agreed to go home with her and to distract her mum so Heather would be able to enter the study unnoticed.
Once that was agreed, the friends had to decide what to do next.

Susan felt that they should watch Amanda and Beverly. They were her two *prime suspects* and the others agreed. The only person who could *spy on* them easily was Arthur. After the fight between Susan and Beverly it was not easy for Susan and her friends to go near Beverly. Arthur, on the other hand, was not known to Beverly. It would not be difficult for him to secretly follow her and watch her movements. If she did have the *locket* she would maybe talk about it to her friends. If Arthur could somehow get near to them in the *playground* or in the school, perhaps he could get some useful information.

Arthur agreed. He was ready to help Susan in any way he could. He thought he would have no problem *spying on* Beverly. He had never really spoken to her and she would not suspect him. There was nothing to link him to Susan. They had been careful not to be seen together, so there was no reason for Beverly to be *suspicious* of him.

Chapter 7: Trouble in the Woods

When their meeting was over they all went back to their classes.

At lunchtime Arthur decided to eat with his friend George as usual. When he entered the canteen he noticed that Beverly, Amanda and some other girls were sitting over by the window. When he collected his lunch from the *serving hatch* he persuaded George to come and sit with him by the window. The table behind Beverly and Amanda was free! Nervously he sat down with his back to the girls. He did not want to attract attention. George was talking about the TV programme he watched last night – 'Eastenders'. It was a soap opera they both loved, but Arthur only half listened. He concentrated hard as he tried to hear the words spoken by the girls.

At one point he was sure he heard them say: "Stupid little *stuck-up*

bitch" and then "who does she think she is?"
It was not clear if they were talking about Susan, but there was obviously some girl at school that they *were out to get*.
After a while, George noticed that Arthur was not really paying attention to him and not eating his lunch.
"*What's up?*" he said.
"Oh, nothing," replied Arthur. "I was just dreaming, that's all."
He still tried to lean back and hear what the girls were saying from time to time, but it was too difficult.

Übung 49: Finde das gesuchte Wort!

ÜBUNG 49 !

1. a table at which you do your schoolwork ____________

2. He tries to stop the ball going in the net. ____________

3. the meal before you go to school ____________

4. You go there if you are injured. ____________

5. the day before today ____________

6. the opposite of interesting ____________

After lunch Arthur told George he had to meet up with the geography teacher. When George had left, Arthur followed Beverly out of the canteen. He kept a safe distance behind her as he did not want to be seen. He followed her down the corridor leading to the gym. That's funny, he thought. There were no gym lessons after lunch, so what was she doing down here? Beverly was acting very *suspiciously*. She looked around to check that no-one was following her. Luckily she had not noticed that Arthur was hiding behind a *pillar*.

All was quiet. Nobody was in the corridor.

Beverly took out her *mobile* and started typing in a message. Who was she *texting*, Arthur wondered, It was not allowed to use *mobile phones* on the school grounds, but many people still did anyway. However, most pupils used their *mobiles* in the *playground* away from the teachers and not indoors. Also why was Beverly on her own away from her friends? It all seemed very *suspicious*.

Arthur stood very still. Beverly was obviously waiting for a reply. She had stopped typing and was just staring at her *mobile*. Suddenly there was a 'peep peep' sound as a new message arrived on her *mobile*. Immediately she typed in a reply, then put the *mobile* back into her handbag.

He looked at his watch to check the time. It was 1.15 p.m. Beverly then hurried back down the corridor. As she passed, Arthur moved slowly around the other side of the *pillar* so as not to be noticed. Fortunately Beverly did not see him.

Susan had spent most of lunchtime *hanging around* in the *playground*. She had not gone into the canteen today and had just eaten some crisps from the snack bar instead. She sat on a *bench* with Tracey under the trees at the edge of the *playground*. From this spot she had a good view over the whole area. In the distance she noticed that Giles was playing football with his *mates*. He did not even see her and she was happy to keep out of his way.

Suddenly she heard the noise 'deedle do da da, deedle do da da': she had a new message on her *mobile*.

Quickly she took it out of her handbag and pressed the 'Read' button.

Tracey leant over to read what it said. The message was short and direct:

"Have *u* got the cash yet?"

Susan turned to Tracey and said:

"What shall I say? Shall I tell them I have it?"
"Sure," said Tracey. "No reason to wait. Let's see what they say."
Susan typed in a short "yes" and pressed the 'Send' button.
It seemed like ages until the answer came back:
"meet us *2nite* @ Bluebell Woods @ 7 p.m. @ picnic area. don't be *l8*! come alone!"
"So!" said Susan. "We have to do the *handover* tonight! At last I get my *locket* back!"
"And we will get the *blackmailers*, too!" said Tracey triumphantly. "They will pay for this!"
Susan typed in a quick message: "ok no *prob* i will be there" and pressed the 'Send' button.
Bluebell Woods was a short walk from the school. It was a popular place at the weekends, but was normally very empty during the day. Susan and her friends knew the area well. There was a big picnic site in the middle of the woods with a *playground*. They often went there to get away from the noise of the city.

Übung 50: Schreibe die Wörter in Großbuchstaben um!

ÜBUNG 50 !

1. Change a letter in CHEST to make a game you play on a board: ______________

2. Take a letter away from CLOSER to make someone who doesn't win: ______________

3. Change a letter from WOOD to make something you can eat: ______________

4. Add a letter to TREE to make a number: ______________

5. Change a letter in STOP to make a place where you can buy things: ____________

6. Find a word that rhymes with CHIPS to make part of your face: ____________

At that moment another text message came on Susan's phone: "Meet me by the bins now I have news." It was from Arthur.
Susan looked up and saw him standing over by the school exit. He did not wave to her, but started walking over to the bins. Obviously he did not want anyone to see him talking to them.
"Come on, Tracey," said Susan. "Let's see what he wants. And get Heather, too."
Tracey walked across the *playground* and found Heather. She told her what was going on and they all met behind the bins in their secret meeting place.
"So, *what's up?*" asked Susan.
Arthur explained how he had just seen Beverly sending a text message.
"And I have just received a message!" explained Susan. "So it must be Beverly who took the *locket*!"
"Just a moment," said Tracey. "What if Beverly is not working alone? I mean this is a big plan to carry out by herself. She is not that clever surely?"
"Yes, I *see* your *point*," said Susan. "Maybe we should hand over the money as planned and then we can see if she is working alone. If we approach her now maybe she will alarm the rest of her gang and the *locket* will be gone forever."
The others agreed.
"Well," said Arthur. "So what's the plan? How are we going to

arrange the *handover* and catch Beverly with her gang, if there is one?"
"They told me to go alone," said Susan. "But I really don't feel safe going there on my own."
"No way!" said Arthur. "It would be really *foolish* to go there alone."

Übung 51: Lies weiter und setze das Gegenteil der Wörter in Klammern ein!

ÜBUNG 51

"We will be with you all the way," said Tracey and Heather.
"And don't (1. remember) f__________ George," said Arthur. "He is a really (2. weak) s__________ *guy* and could be very useful if there is any trouble."
So the four friends agreed to meet at the back of Susan's house at 6 p.m. From there they could go on their bikes to Bluebell Woods. Each of them was to (3. take) b__________ their share of the money in cash and Arthur said he would borrow the rest (4. to) f__________ his dad. Susan would carry the money in a plastic *pouch*, which she could hang around her neck. After they had agreed the plan, they all (5. came) w__________ separately across the *playground* and back to their classes.

It was raining when they all *gathered* around the back of Susan's

house. They had all brought their waterproof jackets. *Despite* the weather they had no choice but to carry out their plan. By meeting around the back of the house they could *avoid* being seen from the main road. They agreed that Susan should leave first and the others would follow in pairs: Arthur with Heather and George with Tracey. Susan was very grateful to George for agreeing to help them. He was a tall strong *lad* and it felt good to have him with them.
When they were all ready, Susan *set off* on her bike towards Bluebell Woods. As soon as she was out of sight, Arthur followed with Heather. George and Tracey waited until they could no longer see the others and then they too jumped on their bikes and cycled towards the woods.
Susan felt very nervous as she approached the woods. It was good to know her friends were behind her, but it still felt strange as she could not see them. Although it was raining it was still light when she entered the woods. She *rode* up the hill that led towards the picnic spot. As she got towards the top of the woods she had to get off and push her bike, as it was very *steep*.

She kept looking around to see if anyone was watching her. A few times she thought she heard a noise in the trees nearby and turned around quickly, but she could not see anyone.
She stopped several times on her walk up the hill. She wanted to make sure that her friends had enough time to catch up with her.
The plan was that Arthur and Heather would hide their bikes at the edge of the woods and then walk up through the trees to the picnic site. By not using the path they hoped they would not be seen.
Tracey and George also walked up through the trees and used a route that came in from the other side.
Susan had to make sure that her friends were all in position before she arrived at the picnic spot. She did not know how many people

would be waiting for her. She was a little bit afraid.
Finally Susan reached the picnic spot. There was nobody there. Slowly she walked over to the table in the centre and walked around it casually. From the corner of her eye she looked into the trees around the picnic spot for signs of her friends. Suddenly she saw the familiar sight of Heather giving her a small wave from behind one of the trees. Then she saw that Tracey was also hiding on the other side of the picnic area.
She was scared when she suddenly heard the ring tone of her phone: 'deedle do da da, deedle do da da'.
"*r u* there?" came the message.
"Yes," Susan typed back.
"Wait!" came the reply.
She sat on the picnic table and waited. It was very hard to keep cool and be patient. What was going on? Where were the *blackmailers*?

Übung 52: Lies weiter und setze das passende Wort ein!
(towards, mopeds, impossible, loud, figures, run, braked, table)

ÜBUNG 52 !

A (1.) ______________ noise alarmed her and she jumped down from the (2.) ______________. The sound of engines roared through the trees. Then two (3.) ______________ with riders rode onto the grass in the picnic area. Normally mopeds were not allowed in the woods, but the two riders obviously did not care. They rode their mopeds straight towards Susan and (4.) ______________ in front of her. The two (5.) ______________ were wearing dark motorbike helmets with the *visors* down. It was (6.) ______________ to see who they were. They were also both wearing black leather jackets. With another loud roar two more mopeds rode into the picnic area from behind. The riders stopped the engines and walked over (7.) ______________ Susan. She was surrounded. She was very frightened, but had to be brave and not (8.) ______________ away.

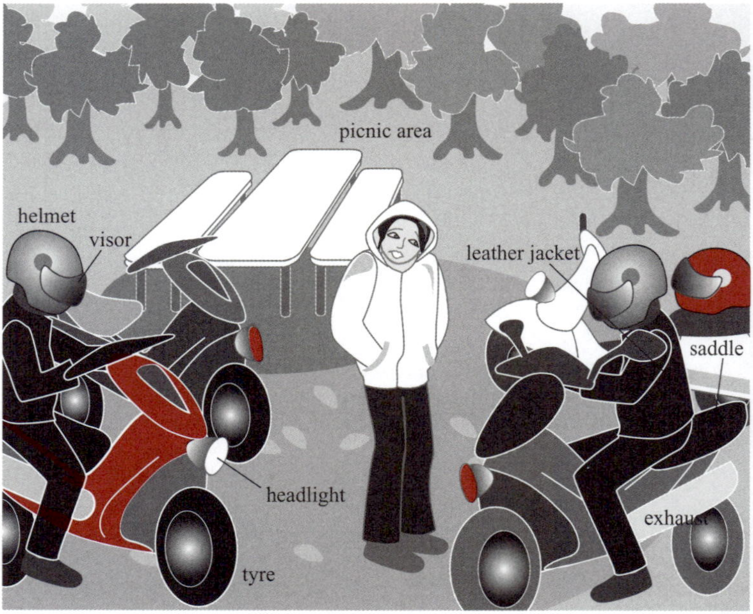

"So, where is the cash?" said one of the figures. He was a young boy with a deep voice. Nobody she recognized. If she handed over the money they might just leave.
"Show me the *locket* first!" she said. "No *locket*, no cash."
"Sure, here it is!" said another of the figures. The figure unzipped the side pocket of his leather jacket and took out Susan's beloved

locket. She ran towards him and tried to grab it.
Another figure stepped in front of her and pushed her back.
"Now where is the cash?" he growled.
Susan's fingers trembled as she reached into her coat and took out the plastic *pouch*.
"Here, take it. It's all there," she said as she pushed the *pouch* towards the figure demanding the money. He grabbed the *pouch* and quickly counted the notes.
"Yep," he said. "All there! Okay *guys*, let's get out of here."
Suddenly Susan realized that they had no intention of returning her *locket*. She had been tricked! In her desperation she dived onto the *guy* holding the *pouch* and knocked it from his hands. He pushed her to the ground and as she fell she shouted out to her friends.
"Help! Help!"
At this signal her friends came running out of their hiding places in the trees.
"Attack, attack!" cried Arthur as he came *rushing* through the trees towards the *guy* who had held the *locket*. He pushed him with both hands and he fell to the ground. The *guy* next to him turned on Arthur and grabbed him around the neck. At that moment George came running from the other side. He grabbed the helmet of the *guy* holding Arthur and pulled him over backwards.
"Leave us alone!" screamed Susan. She had now got up again and joined in the fight, kicking and *pounding* her *fists* against the attackers.
The *guy* with the *locket* had managed to get to his feet. He jumped on his moped and wanted to ride off, but at that moment Tracey came running out of the trees and tried to block his way. He *swerved* to *avoid* her, but then with a *sickening thud* the moped crashed into Tracey, throwing her to the ground. She let out a scream of pain and then went silent. She lay *bleeding* on the ground.

Susan *rushed* over to where Tracey was lying.
"She's *unconscious*!" she cried. "Help, somebody help me!"
Heather and Arthur came running over to where Susan was *kneeling* beside Tracey.
George was still trying to *fight off* the other attackers, but he *was outnumbered*. They had knocked him to the ground and kicked him as he lay on the ground.

ÜBUNG 53 !

Übung 53: Welche Wörter gehören zusammen? Ordne zu!

1. ☐ to score	a) annoyed
2. ☐ to ease	b) a secret
3. ☐ to take	c) a goal
4. ☐ to be	d) care
5. ☐ to keep	e) sense
6. ☐ to ride	f) the pain
7. ☐ to get	g) a bicycle
8. ☐ to make	h) dressed

"Come on! Let's get out of here!" one of the voices said. The other figures got on their mopeds and rode off out of the woods.
Susan was in a state of shock and did not know what to do.
"We need to call an ambulance!" said Arthur. "We need to get help!"
Susan just nodded. She was shaking from shock.
"Give me your phone!" said Arthur. Quickly, he called an ambulance. Then he looked up and noticed that George was lying on the ground and *groaning*.
"Heather, go over and *check on* George!" he shouted.
Heather did as he said and ran over to where George was lying.
"He's hurt," she said. She leant over him and tried to *comfort* him.

"Help is coming," she said. "We have called for an ambulance!" Gently she *stroked* his head to *reassure* him. She took off her coat and put it over him to keep him warm and dry.

Übung 54: Lies weiter und unterstreiche die sieben Adjektive im Text!

ÜBUNG 54 !

Susan and Arthur had done the same for Tracey and had covered her with their coats. Arthur checked that she was breathing, but they were afraid to move her. They had both done first aid at school and remembered that it was not wise to move an injured body. There may be *internal injuries* or broken bones. Susan was shaking from shock and Arthur put his hand around her to *comfort* her. He called over to where Heather was and said:
"Help is on its way! The ambulance will be here very soon."
The ground was very *muddy* and Tracey looked badly hurt. She lay on her back in the grass. Arthur moved away the branches and made the *space* around her so that the ambulance men would be able to reach her better.

Susan *was overcome with tears*.
"It's all my fault!" she cried. "It's all my fault! If I had not got you all involved none of this would have happened. And now Tracey is badly hurt. She may even die!"
"Calm down!" said Arthur, taking control. "She is not going to die. She is just *unconscious*, that's all. Don't worry; help is on its way. And Susan – it isn't your fault! We all wanted to help you, remember? The only fault is with those cruel *guys* on the mopeds. Who were they? Did you recognize anybody?"
"No," replied Susan. "With those helmets and the black jackets it

was not possible. I didn't recognize any of their voices either."
"Well, the important thing is that we get Tracey to hospital as soon as possible. We can deal with the rest later," said Arthur.
Yes, thought Susan. All that mattered was that Tracey was all right. She could not even think about what she would do if anything happened to Tracey. She looked across at Heather. Heather was trying to be brave and not cry, but Susan could see that she was very shocked and *upset*. She called over to her:
"How is George doing?"
"He is conscious!" cried Heather. "But he is in a lot of pain. I think he may have broken his shoulder!"
"Oh no!" said Susan. "Those *guys* were really rough, weren't they?"
Her words were interrupted by the sound of a siren in the distance. Then they saw a blue flashing light as an ambulance drove slowly up the hill. It stopped at the edge of the picnic area. Three men got out and raced over to where Tracey was laying. Susan pointed across to where George was, as well. Two of them stayed with Tracey and the other ran over to *check on* George.
The ambulance men soon decided that both the injured teenagers would have to go to hospital. They *radioed* for another ambulance, which came shortly afterwards, followed by a police car.
Tracey had to be carried into the ambulance on a *stretcher*. They asked if Susan wanted to go with her and she agreed.

! ÜBUNG 55

Übung 55: Lies weiter und setze die Verben in der richtigen Zeitform ein!

Heather (1. stay) ____________ with George and rode in the ambulance with him, while Arthur (2. ride) ____________ in the police car.

He (3. want) ______________ to go to the hospital, too, but the policeman (4. say) ______________ it was better if they accompanied him. He (5. give) ______________ them the personal details of George and the phone numbers of their parents, too.

As the ambulance (6. drive) ______________ down the hill, Susan (7. sit) ______________ and (8. hold) ______________ Tracey's hand.

It had been an incredible evening. It had all gone so badly wrong. She did not care about her *locket* anymore. The only thing that she cared about was that Tracey should *recover*. She began to cry and the ambulance men *comforted* her.
"Don't worry," they said. "She will be fine."
They were giving Tracey oxygen and she was breathing slowly. It looked horrible to Susan, but the *paramedics* assured her that everything was okay and all her body functions were normal. They had cleaned up the cuts on her face and she looked a lot better.
For Arthur it was the first time he had been in a police car. In some ways he was actually quite excited, but he was worried about the others and kept asking the police questions. Eventually they agreed to take him to the hospital as well, but first they took him home to see his parents. His mum and dad were of course very shocked and had lots of questions, but the police were able to *reassure* them and to keep them calm.
When they finally got to the hospital Tracey had *regained consciousness*. She was sitting up in the bed with a bandage on her head and looked much better. Her parents were with her and Susan refused to leave her bedside. Susan's parents were waiting outside the room as it was too crowded inside.

Once Arthur was sure Tracey was okay, he went into the room next door where George was.

"How are you feeling?" he asked. George too was sitting up in bed and his shoulder was bandaged.

"It's just a bad *sprain*," he said. "Luckily it isn't broken. I have strong bones!"

"Man, you were great!" continued Arthur. "The way you *fought off* those *guys* was *awesome*!"

"Yes, but there were just too many of them. And then they got away with both the *locket* and the cash!" said George, disappointed. "We should have jumped on them sooner!"

"Don't worry," said Arthur. "The police are sure to catch them sooner or later."

The two of them sat chatting for another half hour until eventually the nurse said that Arthur would have to leave. He said goodnight to his friend and was driven home by Tracey's parents.

ÜBUNG 56 !

Übung 56: Wähle das passende Wort aus und unterstreiche es!

1. Arthur hid/slept in the bushes.
2. The blackmailer demanded/wished the money.
3. The phone called/rang.
4. Susan's friends hit/helped her.
5. The gang fought/spoke with George.
6. Chess is quick/quiet.
7. The four friends agreed/argued to meet at Susan's house.
8. Tracey had to be caught/carried into the ambulance on a stretcher.
9. It's all Susan's fault/fool.
10. Susan and her friends new/knew the area well.

Chapter 8: Justice is Done

Susan awoke early the next morning and lay in her bed thinking about everything that had happened the night before. It all seemed like a bad dream. But at least Tracey was being looked after now. Both Tracey and George had spent the night at the hospital under observation.

Übung 57: Lies weiter und ergänze den Text mit ***she, her, they*** *oder* ***them****.*

ÜBUNG 57 !

Her parents had said that Susan could stay home from school, so (1.) ________ did not have to get up early. (2.) ________ mum said that Susan should take a *rest* and that (3.) ________ would write (4.) ________ a *sick note*. They were very pleased that Susan was not injured. When she told (5.) ________ that her *locket* was stolen, she was very surprised that they did not even get angry. (6.) ________ were more concerned over the *blackmail* and the fight in Bluebell Woods. How silly she had been not to trust (7.) ________, she thought. (8.) ________ should have gone to (9.) ________ straight-away.

Halfway through breakfast, suddenly the doorbell rang and her mum was surprised and got up to answer it. She came back with a concerned look on her face. “It’s the police, dear,” she said. “They want to ask you a few questions.”

“No problem,” said Susan confidently. “Show them in.”
The police asked about how the *locket* had been stolen and then about the text messages that Susan had received. They said they would have to take her phone away with them and maybe they would be able to trace the sender of the messages. Good idea, thought Susan. That had not occurred to her. They wanted a full description of the *locket* and details of the moped riders.
“Thank you very much, you have been very helpful. You were very lucky that no-one else was hurt,” they said. “In future, don’t *take* such *risks* and contact the police straightaway.”

ÜBUNG 58 !

Übung 58: Lies weiter und finde für jedes der Wörter in Klammern das passende Reimwort!

Susan agreed and promised that she would not (1. cry) ____________ to act without telling her parents next time. She hoped that there would never (2. tree) ____________ a next time! She did not want to go through such a nightmare ever again!

Once they (3. mad) ____________ finished interviewing Susan, the police *constables* visited the homes of all the (4. mother) ____________ teenagers, too. They were very serious in their investigation and (5. look) ____________ notes of everything that the five friends (6. hold) ____________ them. They also asked the parents questions, but of course they (7. hit) ____________ not know anything of what had happened and had been *left in the dark*.

Eventually when they had left, Susan caught the bus to the local hospital to visit Tracey.
When she arrived, Tracey was sitting up in bed reading a magazine. "I'm bored!" she said. "When can I get out of here? The nurses are nice, but there's nothing to do really. And you can't even use your phone!"

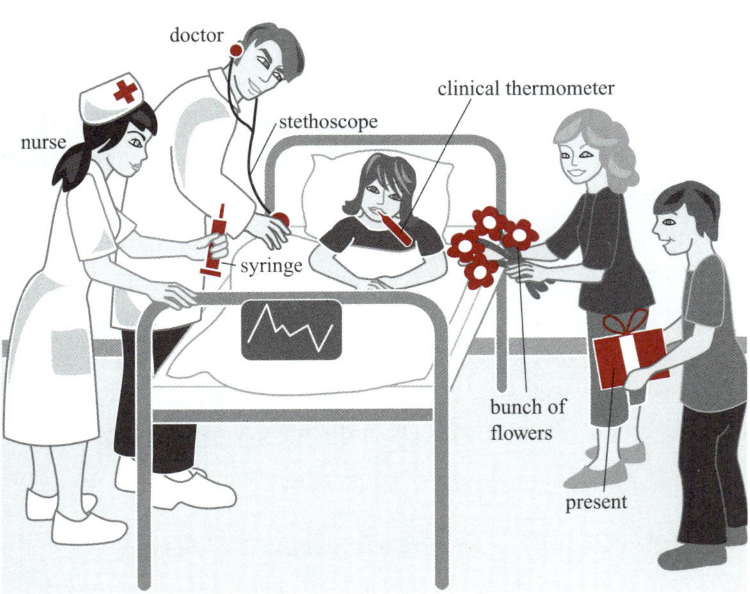

"Heather sends her love," said Susan. "She is sorry she is not able to come in today, but I think she is still in shock. Her mum rang me. She said Heather was sick in the night and has to stay in bed, poor thing."
After a while Susan felt that Tracey was obviously much better, so she went next door to visit George.
George looked up when Susan entered his room. What a pretty girl

she was! He could see now why Arthur was so *keen* on her.

Susan walked up to the side of his bed.

"Thank you for what you did!" she said, looking him straight in the eyes. "You were really brave yesterday. How can I ever repay you?"

"Oh, it was nothing," he answered with a big smile. "That's what friends are for. Arthur told me you were in trouble and I was only too glad to help."

Susan lent over and *gave* him *a* little *hug*, making sure not to press his injured shoulder.

George went bright red. He was not used to being *hugged* by girls.

Susan thanked him again and made her way back to Tracey's bed to chat about the events of last night all over again. She also had to tell her all about the visit of the police *constables*.

About half an hour later Arthur arrived at the hospital as well. He too had been given permission to stay off school that day.

"*Due to* the shock," he said and laughed.

"Thank you so much!" Susan said and *gave* Arthur *a* big *hug*, too. She was so pleased that it was all over and that her friends were together again. She seemed to want to *hug* everyone today.

ÜBUNG 59 !

Übung 59: Setze die richtigen Verben in die Lücken ein!
(blushed, murmured, made, stay, check, wounded, go, enjoyed)

Arthur (1.) ____________, but secretly he (2.) ____________ being *hugged* by Susan. He hoped this would not be the last time either.

After a short time Arthur announced that he would (3.) ____________ next door to (4.) ____________ on George.

"I'm sure he's getting lonely!" he (5.) ____________. Really he would rather have stayed with Susan, but he knew that it was more important to (6.) ____________ loyal to his friend. After all, he had been (7.) ____________ in action!

Later in the day the doctors (8.) ____________ their rounds and said that both Tracey and George could be *dismissed*.

The next day when they returned to school their classmates were *suspicious*. Why had they missed school, they all wanted to know? And why were all five off sick? And what had happened to Tracey, why was she wearing a *plaster* on her head? They had decided to say that Tracey had been involved in a bicycle accident and George in a fight. (Well, that was true anyway!)

Übung 60: Unterstreiche im folgenden Textabschnitt die Gegenteile der Wörter in Klammern!
(1. earlier, 2. started, 3. up, 4. bad, 5. short, 6. whispered)

ÜBUNG 60 !

Later that day Susan had invited her friends to have dinner with her at her house. Suddenly the doorbell rang and they all stopped talking.
Susan's mum led in two policemen and invited them to sit down.
"Well," they said. "We have some good news. We found the *locket* when we searched Giles' bedroom. We had to apply for a *search warrant*, that is why it took so long. We have *recovered* the cash as well."
"Giles! My ex-boyfriend!" shouted Susan angrily. "That can't be true! He was the one behind this after all? We thought it could not possibly be him!"

The policemen explained how Giles had been working together with a band of thieves. He was not the *ringleader*, but he had led them to Susan and told them about the *locket*. On the day of the hockey match two of the gang had been standing by the *pitch* in the crowd. The other two had gone into the changing room unnoticed and stolen the *locket*. Apparently Giles had persuaded Beverly to help them. He knew she hated Susan and he had promised her a share of the money as well. Beverly had showed the *guys* where Susan's clothes were hanging and made sure no-one saw them steal the *locket*. She also then helped sending the text messages. The police had traced the messages to her phone and she had *confessed* everything when they questioned her.

"So she was involved as well!" said Susan triumphantly.

"And here is your *locket*!" said the policeman.

He hung the *locket* around Susan's neck and Susan held it *tight*. She would not let it out of her sight for a long time. She turned to see her friends standing around her: Heather, Tracey, George and Arthur. She went to each of them and *gave* them *a* big *hug*, but Arthur got the longest one. In her joy she even gave him a kiss as well.

"Wow!" he smiled. "Well, that definitely makes my day!"

George turned to Heather, put his arm around her and said, "Mine too!"

"What about me?" asked Tracey and they all joined together in a big group hug. All their problems had now been solved and they were one happy band of five!

Abschlusstest

Übung 1: Wähle das passende Wort für jeden Satz aus und unterstreiche es!

1. She went/waited through the crowd.
2. I become/get my pocket money tomorrow.
3. Where/Were is he now?
4. Are/Our car is muddy.
5. There/Their she is at last.
6. Arthur is sweat/sweet on Susan.

Übung 2: Setze die Verben ins Simple Past!

1. She (ring) ________________ her mother.
2. We (bring) ________________ the money.
3. I (twist) ________________ him round my little finger.
4. They (sleep) ________________ very badly.
5. We (catch) ________________ the ball every time.
6. You (ride) ________________ your bike to the park.

Übung 3: Welches Wort ist das „schwarze Schaf“?

1. goalkeeper, referee, player, ball
2. ambush, blackmail, paramedic, theft
3. trap, limp, crawl, tiptoe

4. talk, speak, hear, mumble
5. sun, fall, rain, snow
6. locket, look, spot, see

Übung 4: Ordne die Buchstaben zu einem sinnvollen Wort!

1. Tracey (diel) ____________ to her father.
2. The shopping centre was full of (sposh) ____________.
3. (samth) ____________ is my favourite subject.
4. Her father (nosred) ____________ loudly every night.
5. She (sturb) ____________ into tears.
6. She ate in the school (teenanc) ____________.
7. A school jacket is called a (rablze) ____________.

Übung 5: Setze die richtigen Präpositionen ein!

1. We are meeting ______ the park.
2. She was the captain ______ the hockey team.
3. She was determined ______ score.
4. I had forgotten ______ the pain.
5. He had fancied her ______ a long time.
6. What is ______ telly?
7. She stared ______ the ceiling.

Übung 6: Ergänze die Begriffe!

1. If you have no money, you are _ r _ k _.
2. A _ o _ st _ _ l _ is a policeman.
3. You hang your clothes in a w _ r _ r _ b _.
4. A p _ u _ h is a kind of bag.
5. Part of a helmet is a _ i _ o _.

Übung 7: Finde für jedes Wort in Klammern das passende Reimwort!

1. He (look) ________________ the locket.
2. Her mother always (books) ________________ the breakfast.
3. He (kid) ________________ in the bushes.
4. (Man) ________________ you get the money?
5. She didn't know his (came) ________________.
6. (Think) ________________ your coke.
7. (Bell) ________________ done!

Übung 8: Sind die folgenden Aussagen wahr? Markiere mit richtig ✔ oder falsch – !

1. Tracey thought Heather was a witch. ☐
2. Susan was a substitute at the hockey game. ☐

3. Giles was Susan's ex-boyfriend. ☐
4. You can have bath in your bed. ☐
5. Ambulances have stretchers in them. ☐
6. Susan met her friends in the park. ☐

Übung 9: Welche Wörter gehören in die Lücken?
(savings, park, escalators, mind, goal)

1. She scored a ______________.

2. ______________ are quicker than stairs.

3. Put the money in your ______________ book.

4. The swings are in the ______________.

5. I have changed my ______________.

Übung 10: Schreibe die Wörter in Großbuchstaben um!

1. Change a letter in RAIN to make something that hurts: ________
2. Add a letter to SORE to get a goal: ______________
3. Change a letter in MOVE to mean a larger amount: ___________
4. Take a letter away from FAST to mean not thin: ______________
5. Add a letter to CARE to mean frighten: ______________
6. Take a letter away from HEAR to make a possessive pronoun: ______________
7. Add a letter to SAD to mean spoken: ______________
8. Change a letter in FOOL to make a part of the body: __________

Übung 11: Wie lauten die Wörter in der richtigen Reihenfolge? Bilde sinnvolle Sätze!

1. too stretched Susan had far and her torn out a leg muscle

2. cheeks down streaming tears the now Susan's were

3. savings out and she her desk took her opened book

4. a blank stared on with his Susan expression Arthur face at

5. band had working Giles with been a of thieves together

Lösungen

Übung 1: 1. gole (goal) 2. aut (out) 3. rite (right) 4. paine (pain) 5. fellt (felt) 6. teers (tears)
Übung 2: 1. the 2. make 3. have 4. felt 5. leg 6. pain 7. water
Übung 3: 1. hold 2. play 3. help 4. appear 5. try Lösung: happy
Übung 4: 1. apple 2. win 3. anger 4. left 5. terrible 6. shoe 7. new
Übung 5: 1. sat 2. cried 3. put 4. tried 5. said 6. helped 7. were
Übung 6: 1. She goes to St. Mary's High School. 2. Her best friends are Heather and Tracey. 3. He is caring. 4. Her grandmother gave her the locket. 5. She blew the whistle.
Übung 7: 1. my 2. their 3. my 4. her 5. his 6. our 7. her 8. his
Übung 8: 1. falls 2. sings 3. runs 4. runs 5. falls 6. sings
Übung 9: 1. June is hotter than January. 2. Running is faster than walking. 3. Russian is more difficult than English. 4. A hockey stick is longer than a tennis racquet. 5. A house is bigger than a flat. 6. A grandmother is older than a mother.
Übung 10: 1. hurt 2. thinks 3. mobile 4. blew 5. looked 6. much
Übung 11: 1. match 2. arms 3. want 4. leg 5. under 6. door 7. come 8. said
Übung 12: 1. c 2. d 3. f 4. e 5. a 6. b
Übung 13: 1. b 2. b 3. c 4. a 5. c
Übung 14: 1. falsch 2. falsch 3. richtig 4. falsch 5. richtig 6. falsch 7. richtig
Übung 15: 1. to 2. out 3. to 4. out 5. for 6. to 7. for
Übung 16: 1. She kept it on her bedside table. 2. They went to the shopping centre to investigate the first suspect Giles. 3. She pounded them with her fists. 4. She rubbed ointment on Susan's leg. 5. Susan's hair is blonde. 6. No, she finished with him.
Übung 17: 1. thing 2. feet 3. time 4. explode 5. locket
Übung 18: 1. slowly 2. difficult 3. closer/nearer 4. small/little 5. long
Übung 19: 1. laughed 2. was 3. felt 4. continued 5. was 6. rose 7. lost
Übung 20: 1. of 2. to 3. out 4. on 5. over
Übung 21: 1. blazer 2. substitute 3. exhausted 4. precious 5. anxious 6. split 7. yawn

Übung 22: 1. d 2. e 3. c 4. b 5. f 6. a
Übung 23: 1. thaught (thought) 2. runing (running) 3. fin (fine) 4. kno (know) 5. shure (sure) 6. tim (time)
Übung 24: 1. The team beat us every time. 2. The sun shone. 3. He was suspicious. 4. They were annoyed. 5. He came to the park every week. 6. We had a message. 7. They won the match.
Übung 25: 1. sat 2. thought 3. spoke 4. sent 5. came 6. grabbed
Übung 26: 1. a 2. An 3. a 4. the 5. a 6. the 7. an 8. the 9. the
Übung 27: 1. She fell into the arms of her mum. 2. The mobile was by her bedside. 3. You can come in now. 4. Who sent the message? 5. I need a bit of space now. 6. Do not tell anyone! 7. She was starting to get annoyed.
Übung 28: 1. d 2. a 3. c 4. b 5. f 6. e 7. h 8. i 9. g
Übung 29: 1. would-be 2. hot 3. big 4. traditional 5. great 6. small 7. round 8. good
Übung 30: 1. sixteen 2. sixty-nine 3. one third 4. one thousand five hundred 5. two million 6. fourth 7. one hundred and ten 8. eighty 9. fifty-three 10. forty-six
Übung 31: 1. noticed 2. cried out 3. definitely 4. normally 5. got up 6. find out
Übung 32: 1. b 2. a 3. b 4. a 5. b
Übung 33: 1. She did nothing because fear kept her from moving. 2. She was hurt on her head and face. 3. They wanted to take her to the hospital. 4. Amanda is Beverly's friend. 5. No, she doesn't want them to know.
Übung 34: 1. f 2. d 3. a 4. g 5. c 6. b 7. e
Übung 35: 1. tolking (talking) 2. to (too) 3. wos (was) 4. stealed (stolen) 5. sad (said) 6. sware (swear) 7. beleive (believe) 8. where (were)
Übung 36: 1. went 2. found 3. saw 4. told 5. lost 6. did 7. said 8. knew
Übung 37: 1. Heather is a good friend of Susan's. 2. Someone has stolen the locket. 3. Susan scored a goal. 4. Susan felt hope rise. 5. The toffees fell on the floor. 6. Who is Tracey? 7. There has to be an explanation. 8. She sent a text message.
Übung 38: 1. a 2. b 3. a 4. b
Übung 39: 1. cook 2. park 3. locket 4. night 5. pound 6. bed

Übung 40: 1. richtig 2. richtig 3. falsch 4. richtig 5. falsch 6. falsch
Übung 41: 1. hockey 2. crowd 3. shoulder 4. blackmailed 5. present 6. uniform 7. anonymous 8. yawned
Übung 42: 1. her 2. his 3. she 4. him 5. her
Übung 43: 1. Has she found the money? 2. Have you tried another jeweller? 3. Have they been to the billiard café? 4. Have I seen the locket before? 5. Has it disappeared from your bag? 6. Have we met the boy? 7. Has she told her parents? 8. Has he received a message? 9. Have you bought a new pair of hockey boots?
Übung 44: 1. How 2. Who 3. Which 4. How 5. When 6. Where 7. What 8. Who
Übung 45: 1. He wanted two hundred pounds. 2. The locket was stolen during the hockey match. 3. Arthur and George helped them. 4. Giles is Susan's ex-boyfriend. 5. Tracey's dad lends her twenty pounds.
Übung 46: 1. alternative 2. nightmare 3. tiptoe 4. duvet 5. magazine 6. purse 7. torch 8. snore
Übung 47: 1. A text message was sent by the blackmailer. 2. The money was stolen by Heather. 3. The goal was scored by Susan. 4. She was hated by someone. 5. They were looked after by her parents. 6. Giles was suspected by the girls.
Übung 48: 1. clock 2. car 3. desk 4. drawers 5. pitch 6. teacher 7. swing
Übung 49: 1. desk 2. goalkeeper 3. breakfast 4. hospital 5. yesterday 6. boring
Übung 50: 1. chess 2. loser 3. food 4. three 5. shop 6. lips
Übung 51: 1. forget 2. strong 3. bring 4. from 5. went
Übung 52: 1. loud 2. table 3. mopeds 4. braked 5. figures 6. impossible 7. towards 8. run
Übung 53: 1. c 2. f 3. d 4. a 5. b 6. g 7. h 8. e
Übung 54: 1. afraid 2. wise 3. injured 4. internal 5. broken 6. muddy 7. clear
Übung 55: 1. stayed 2. rode 3. wanted 4. said 5. gave 6. drove 7. sat 8. held
Übung 56: 1. hid 2. demanded 3. rang 4. helped 5. fought 6. quiet 7. agreed 8. carried 9. fault 10. knew

Übung 57: 1. she 2. Her 3. she 4. her 5. them 6. They 7. them 8. She 9. them
Übung 58: 1. try 2. be 3. had 4. other 5. took 6. told 7. did
Übung 59: 1. blushed 2. enjoyed 3. go 4. check 5. murmured 6. stay 7. wounded 8. made
Übung 60: 1. Later 2. stopped 3. down 4. good 5. long 6. shouted

Lösungen Abschlusstest

Übung 1: 1. went 2. get 3. Where 4. Our 5. There 6. sweet
Übung 2: 1. rang 2. brought 3. twisted 4. slept 5. caught 6. rode
Übung 3: 1. ball 2. paramedic 3. trap 4. hear 5. fall 6. locket
Übung 4: 1. lied 2. shops 3. Maths 4. snored 5. burst 6. canteen 7. blazer
Übung 5: 1. in 2. of 3. to 4. about 5. for 6. on 7. at
Übung 6: 1. broke 2. constable 3. wardrobe 4. pouch 5. visor
Übung 7: 1. took 2. cooks 3. hid 4. Can 5. name 6. Drink 7. Well
Übung 8: 1. falsch 2. falsch 3. richtig 4. falsch 5. richtig 6. richtig
Übung 9: 1. goal 2. Escalators 3. savings 4. park 5. mind
Übung 10: 1. pain 2. score 3. more 4. fat 5. scare 6. her 7. said 8. foot
Übung 11: 1. Susan had stretched out her leg too far and torn a muscle. 2. The tears were now streaming down Susan's cheeks. 3. She opened her desk and took out her savings book. 4. Arthur stared at Susan with a blank expression on his face. 5. Giles had been working together with a band of thieves.

Glossar

Abkürzungen im Glossar

fam	*umgangssprachlich*
pl	*Plural*
v	*Verb*

addicted to	abhängig von
amazement	Erstaunen
ambush *v*	überfallen
ambush	Hinterhalt, Überfall
arouse *v* **suspicion**	Verdacht erwecken
ask *v* **sb. out**	jmd. um ein Date bitten
at all costs	um jeden Preis
avoid *v*	vermeiden, meiden
avoid *v* **suspicion**	Verdacht von sich ablenken
awesome	großartig
back *v* **down**	einen Rückzieher machen
be (was, been) *v* **a match for sb.**	jmd. gewachsen sein
be (was, been) *v* **attached to sth.**	an etw. hängen
be (was, been) *v* **fed up**	die Schnauze voll haben *fam*
be (was, been) *v* **fond of sb.**	jmd. mögen
be (was, been) *v* **out to get sb.**	es auf jmd. abgesehen haben
be (was, been) *v* **outnumbered**	in der Minderheit sein
be (was, been) *v* **overcome with tears**	von Tränen überwältigt werden
be (was, been) *v* **sweet on sb.**	auf jmd. stehen
bedside cabinet	Nachtschrank
bench	Bank
better-off	besser dran, wohlhabender
bitch *fam*	Schlampe *fam*

blackmail *v*	erpressen
blackmail	Erpressung
blackmailer	Erpresser(in)
bleed (bled, bled) *v*	bluten
blow (blew, blown) *v* **sth.** *fam*	hier: etw. vermasseln *fam*
blush *v*	erröten
bold	kühn
bother *v*	ärgern, quälen
break-up	Trennung
broke *fam*	hier: pleite *fam*
bruised	verletzt, verschrammt
bully *v*	einschüchtern, tyrannisieren
burst (burst, burst) *v* **into tears**	in Tränen ausbrechen
calf, calves *pl*	hier: Wade
chase *v* **sb.**	jmd. nachlaufen
check *v* **on sb.**	jmd. abchecken *fam*, überprüfen
cheer *v*	jubeln
cheer *v* **sb. up**	jmd. aufmuntern
chest	Brust
chest of drawers	Kommode
chill *v*	sich entspannen
claim *v*	behaupten
clay	Ton
clench *v* **one's fists**	die Fäuste ballen
clench *v* **one's teeth together**	die Zähne zusammenbeißen
comb	Kamm
comfort *v*	beruhigen
compassionate	mitfühlend, voller Mitgefühl
confess *v*	beichten
constable	Polizist(in)
convinced	überzeugt

cope *v* **with sth.**	etw. verkraften, mit etw. klarkommen
courtyard	Hof
crawl *v*	krabbeln, kriechen
creak *v*	knarren
creep (crept, crept) *v*	sich hineinschleichen
cross	verärgert
daft	doof
dare *v*	wagen
date *v* **sb.**	mit jmd. gehen
defender	Verteidiger(in)
deny *v*	abstreiten
despite	trotz
dismiss *v* **sb.**	jmd. entlassen
divert *v* **attention**	Aufmerksamkeit ablenken
done in	erschöpft, fix und fertig
down-to-earth	bodenständig
drawer	Schublade
due to	wegen
dump *v* **sth.**	etw. wegwerfen
dustbin	Mülltonne
duvet	Bettdecke
earplugs *pl*	Ohrenstöpsel
ease *v* **the pain**	den Schmerz lindern
embarrassed	verlegen
embarrassing	peinlich
exhausted	erschöpft
expectantly	erwartungsvoll
eyeball to eyeball	Auge in Auge
face *v* **sth./sb.**	sich etw./jmd. stellen
fancy *v* **sb.**	auf jmd. stehen

fight (fought, fought) *v* **off**	abwehren, ankämpfen gegen
find (found, found) *v* **favour with sb.**	jmd. gefallen
fist	Faust
fling (flung, flung) *v*	werfen
fool *v* **sb.**	jmd. täuschen
foolish	dumm, albern
forgers *pl*	Geldfälscher(innen)
gap	(Tür-)Spalt
gather *v*	(sich ver)sammeln
gaze *v*	angaffen, starren
GCSEs *pl*	brit. Schulabschlussprüfung (mittlere Reife)
genuine	authentisch, aufrichtig
get (got, got) *v* **at sb.**	jmd. angreifen
get (got, got) *v* **on sb.'s nerves**	jmd. nerven
give (gave, given) *v* **sb. a hug**	jmd. umarmen
give (gave, given) *v* **sb. the creeps**	jmd. gruseln, Gänsehaut machen
glimmer of hope	ein Fünkchen Hoffnung
go (went, gone) *v* **out with sb.**	mit jmd. gehen
goalkeeper	Torwart
gravy	Bratensoße
groan *v*	stöhnen
grumpy	schlecht gelaunt
guy	Kerl, Typ
hallway	Flur
handover	Übergabe
hang (hung, hung) *v* **around**	rumhängen
hang (hung, hung) *v* **out**	rumhängen
hate *v* **sb.'s guts**	jmd. nicht ausstehen können

have (had, had) *v* **a crush on sb.**	in jmd. verknallt sein
have (had, had) *v* **a nerve**	frech sein
have (had, had) *v* **a point**	Recht haben
have (had, had) *v* **a soft spot for sb.**	eine Schwäche für jmd. haben
have (had, had) *v* **it in for sb.**	es auf jmd. abgesehen haben
head *v* **(back)**	(zurück)steuern
heirloom	Erbstück
help *v* **sb. to his/her feet**	jmd. hochhelfen
hesitate *v*	zögern
hug *v* **sb.**	jmd. umarmen
humiliated	erniedrigt
internal injuries *pl*	innere Verletzungen
jerk	Trottel
keen	hier: wach, scharf
kneel (knelt, knelt) *v*	knien
lad	Kerl
leave (left, left) *v* **sb. in the dark**	jmd. im Ungewissen lassen
limp *v*	hinken
loads of	viel
loan	Darlehen
locket	Medaillon
lousy	lausig, übel
mad	hier: böse, fies
mansion	Herrenhaus, Villa
mate	Kumpel
mean	gemein, mies
mobile (phone)	Handy
muddy	schlammig
mumble *v*	grummeln
narrow *v*	zusammenkneifen (Augen)

nasty	böse
no point in doing sth.	es hat keinen Sinn, etw. zu tun
nosy	neugierig
nuisance	Ärgernis, Plage
ointment	Salbe
onlookers *pl*	Zuschauer
over the top	übertrieben
ox, oxen *pl*	Ochse
pace	Schritt
paramedic	Sanitäter(in)
pile *v* **on the pressure**	jmd. unter Druck setzen
pillar	Säule
pitch	Spielfeld
plaster	Heftpflaster
playground	Spielplatz
pocket money	Taschengeld
pouch	Beutel
pound *v*	schlagen, hämmern
pressure *v* **sb.**	jmd. drängen
pride	Stolz; stolz
prime suspect	Hauptverdächtige(r)
put (put, put) *v* **the blame on sb.**	den Verdacht auf jmd. lenken
quid *fam*	Pfund (britische Währung)
rack *v* **one's brain**	sich den Kopf zerbrechen
radio *v*	funken
raise *v*	hier: aufbringen, besorgen
real nice	toll, super
reassure *v* **sb.**	jmd. beschwichtigen, beruhigen
recover *v*	wiederfinden; sich erholen
referee	Schiedsrichter(in)

regain *v* **consciousness**	das Bewusstsein wieder-erlangen
relief	Erleichterung
reluctantly	widerstrebend
rely *v* **on sb.**	sich auf jmd. verlassen
rest	hier: Pause, Ruhe
ride (rode, ridden) *v*	fahren (Fahrrad)
ringleader	Bandenführer
rise (rose, risen) *v* **(up)**	hier: aufsteigen
rub *v* **(in)**	(ein)reiben
rush *v*	eilen
sail *v*	segeln, hier: fliegen
savings book	Sparbuch
scare *v* **off**	verschrecken
score *v* **(a goal)**	punkten, (ein Tor) erzielen
search warrant	Durchsuchungsbefehl
see (saw, seen) *v* **the back of sb.**	jmd. los werden
see (saw, seen) *v* **sb.'s point**	jmd. verstehen
serving hatch	Küchendurchreiche
set (set, set) *v* **off**	sich auf den Weg machen
showdown	Auseinandersetzung
sick note	Krankmeldung
sickening thud	scheußlicher, dumpfer Aufschlag
sleeve	Ärmel
snob	Snob
snore *v*	schnarchen
sob *v*	schluchzen
sort *v* **sth. out**	etw. regeln; etw. aussortieren
space	(Frei-)Raum, Platz
split (split, split) *v* **up (with sb.)**	sich von jmd. trennen

sponge	Schwamm
spot *v* **sb.**	jmd. sehen, bemerken
sprain	Verstauchung
spy *v* **(on sb.)**	(jmd. nach)spionieren
squeeze *v*	ausdrücken
stationery	Schreibwaren
steep	steil
steer *v*	etw. lenken, steuern
stern	ernst, streng
stretcher	Tragbahre
stroke *v*	streicheln
stuck-up	hochnäsig
substitute	Ersatzspieler(in)
substitutes' bench	Ersatzbank
suspicious	verdächtig; misstrauisch
sweat *v*	schwitzen
swerve *v*	ausweichen
swing	Schaukel
swot	Streber(in)
tackle *v* **sb.**	mit jmd. fertig werden
take (took, taken) *v* **a risk**	ein Risiko eingehen
team mate	Mitspieler(in)
tear (torn, torn) *v* **a muscle**	einen Muskel zerren
tell (told, told) *v* **sb. off**	jmd. ermahnen, zurechtweisen
telly *fam*	Fernseher
text *v* **sb.**	jmd. eine SMS schreiben
theft	Diebstahl
tight	fest
tiptoe *v*	auf Zehenspitzen gehen
torch	Taschenlampe
trap *v* **sb.**	jmd. fangen, in die Falle locken

turn *v* **on one's heel**	auf dem Absatz kehrtmachen
twist *v* **sb. around one's little finger**	jmd. um den Finger wickeln
unconscious	bewusstlos
upset	verärgert, aufgebracht
valuable	Wertgegenstand; wertvoll
visor	Visier
wardrobe	Kleiderschrank
well-off	vermögend
well up	sehr wohl
whack	schlagend
What a cheek!	Was für eine Frechheit!
What's up?	Was ist los?
wind (wound, wound) *v* **sb. up**	jmd. ärgern
wipe *v*	wischen
witch	Hexe
withdraw (withdrew, withdrawn) *v*	abheben (Geld)
would-be	vermeintlich
yawn *v*	gähnen
yob	Halbstarker, Rowdy

Teenage-Talk-Glossar

ask *v* **sb. out**	jmd. um ein Date bitten
awesome	großartig
be (was, been) *v* **fed up**	die Schnauze voll haben
be (was, been) *v* **sweet on sb.**	auf jmd. stehen
bitch	Schlampe
blow (blew, blown) *v* **sth.**	hier: etw. vermasseln

broke	hier: pleite
chill *v*	sich entspannen
daft	doof
done in	erschöpft, fix und fertig
fancy *v* **sb.**	auf jmd. stehen
get (got, got) *v* **at sb.**	jmd. angreifen
get (got, got) *v* **on sb.'s nerves**	jmd. nerven
give (gave, given) *v* **sb. the creeps**	jmd. gruseln, Gänsehaut machen
go (went, gone) *v* **out with sb.**	mit jmd. gehen
grumpy	schlecht gelaunt
guy	Kerl, Typ
hang (hung, hung) *v* **around**	rumhängen
hang (hung, hung) *v* **out**	rumhängen
have (had, had) *v* **a crush on sb.**	in jmd. verknallt sein
jerk	Trottel
lad	Kerl
lousy	lausig, übel
mate	Kumpel
nosy	neugierig
snob	Snob
real nice	toll
split (split, split) *v* **up**	sich von jmd. trennen
stuck-up	hochnäsig
swot	Streber
text *v* **sb.**	jmd. eine SMS schreiben
What's up?	Was ist los?
wind (wound, wound) *v* **sb. up**	jmd. ärgern
yob	Halbstarker, Rowdy

SMS-Glossar

@ (at)	um, bei, an
2 (to/too)	zu; auch
2day (today)	heute
2moro (tomorrow)	morgen
2nite (tonight)	heute Abend
b4 (before)	vorher
c u 2moro (see you tomorrow)	wir sehen uns morgen
c u l8r (see you later)	bis später
gr8 (great)	toll
l8 (late)	spät
lol (lots of love)	viele liebe Grüße
c yr (see your)	siehe dein
no1 (no-one)	niemand
pls (please)	bitte
prob (problem)	Problem
r u (are you)	bist du
thx (thanks)	danke
txt bk (text back)	zurückschreiben (SMS)
u (you)	du
u r (you are)	du bist
u want 2 (you want to)	willst du
w8 (wait)	warten
yr (your)	dein/ihr